INSPIRING
PROGRESS

Other Norton/Worldwatch Books

State of the World 1984 through *2006*
An annual report on progress toward a sustainable society

Vital Signs 1992 through *2003, 2005, and 2006*
An annual report on the environmental trends that are shaping our future

Saving the Planet
Lester R. Brown
Christopher Flavin
Sandra Postel

How Much Is Enough?
Alan Thein Durning

Last Oasis
Sandra Postel

Full House
Lester R. Brown
Hal Kane

Power Surge
Christopher Flavin
Nicholas Lenssen

Who Will Feed China?
Lester R. Brown

Tough Choices
Lester R. Brown

Fighting for Survival
Michael Renner

The Natural Wealth of Nations
David Malin Roodman

Life Out of Bounds
Chris Bright

Beyond Malthus
Lester R. Brown
Gary Gardner
Brian Halweil

Pillar of Sand
Sandra Postel

Vanishing Borders
Hilary French

Eat Here
Brian Halweil

INSPIRING PROGRESS

Religions' Contributions to Sustainable Development

Gary T. Gardner

W·W·NORTON & COMPANY

NEW YORK   LONDON

Copyright © 2006 by Worldwatch Institute
1776 Massachusetts Avenue, NW
Washington, DC 20036
www.worldwatch.org

The text of this book is composed in Berkeley Book, with the display set in Scala Sans.
Cover and interior designed by Lyle Rosbotham; manufacturing by The Maple-Vail
Book Manufacturing Group

First Edition
ISBN-13: 978-0-393-32832-5
ISBN-10: 0-393-32832-5

W. W. Norton & Company, Inc., 500 Fifth Avenue, New York, N.Y. 10110
www.wwnorton.com

W. W. Norton & Company Ltd., Castle House, 75/76 Wells Street, London W1T 3QT

1 2 3 4 5 6 7 8 9 0

For Mom and Dad,
  who planted the vision,
For Sally,
  who waters it daily,
For Sam and Clara,
  who will reap the fruit:
A just and sustainable world.

Contents

Figures

Tables

Sidebars

Acknowledgments

The religious and sustainability communities are filled with committed and generous people who were wonderfully helpful to me in this project.

I am particularly grateful to the Trustees of the V. Kann Rasmussen Foundation for their leadership in building bridges between the two communities and for the generous funding that made this project possible. The Rasmussen Trustees grasp a vital truth: values shape policies and practices, and religions are a major force in defining the dominant values of many societies.

I am especially indebted to Mary Evelyn Tucker and Martin Palmer for their kindness and direction with my work on the nexus between religion and sustainability over the years. Each is a visionary leader in the effort to engage religions on sustainability issues, and the work of each has shaped mine. Special thanks also to Jim Burke, whose careful and insightful questions helped sharpen the book's focus.

I am also grateful to those who generously gave their time to sit for interviews, including Matthew Anderson-Stembridge, Eduardo Athayde, Rev. Jim Ball, Joy Bergey, Rev. Sally Bingham, Rev. Dave Bookless, Sr. Diane Cardiff, Cassandra Carmichael, Tony Deamer, Rabbi Fred Dobbs, Paul Gorman, David Hallman, Gerald Iversen, Andy Rudin, and Sr. Pat Wolf. Many of these individuals also read parts of the manuscript and gave excellent comments and corrections. Others who kindly reviewed chapters include Erik Assadourian, Martin Bauschke, Tom Dewan, Tee

Gardner, Richard Gray, Brian Halweil, Danielle Nierenberg, Tom Prugh, and Mary Redfern.

The Worldwatch Institute is full of bright researchers whose work I have drawn on throughout the book. Chapter 2 in particular benefited from the vision of Ed Ayres and from research done by Erik Assadourian, Lisa Mastny, Michael Renner, Payal Sampat, Radhika Sarin, and Janet Sawin. Chapter 7 relied heavily on research originally provided by Erik Assadourian. To all of my colleagues, I am deeply grateful.

Lisa Mastny edited the work quickly and with great precision, and her excellent management skills kept the production process on schedule. I am grateful for her guidance, and for Lyle Rosbotham's creative magic with the book's design. I also appreciate the hard work of Worldwatch's Communications Manager, Darcey Rakestraw, and Director of Marketing, Patricia Shyne, in getting the message out to a wide audience.

I owe a special note of thanks to my parents, Tom and Tee Gardner, who planted in me both the seeds of faith and the desire to build a better world, the combination of which is represented in this book. I am grateful for their love and guidance.

Finally, I would like to thank my wife, Sally, and my children, Sam and Clara, for releasing me from family duties for many months as the book was finished. Their patience with my absence has been extraordinary, and without their forbearance this book would not have been completed. They have my heartfelt gratitude and love.

Gary Gardner
Grass Valley, California
May 2006

Introduction

*"Fundamental progress has to do with
the reinterpretation of basic ideas."*
—Alfred North Whitehead[1]*

Tony Deamer is an entrepreneur, inventor, and civic leader, a dynamo of progress in Vanuatu, a small island nation in the South Pacific. He runs a car dealership and an air charter service in the capital city of Port Vila, with 18 employees between the two businesses. He is developing a new kind of fuel to power the cars of Vanuatu. And he serves on the board of a local Bahá'í school and as president of the national Red Cross. Deamer cuts a familiar profile: millions of go-getters like him worldwide provided the financial capital, technological innovation, and civic leadership that generated unprecedented societal advances in the 20th century, advances that made the century synonymous with the word "progress."

But look closer and it's clear Deamer's activities have an added, 21st-century twist. His innovative "Island Fuel" is made from coconut oil, which burns more cleanly than petroleum—a reflection of his desire to "leave something behind for my kids, some hope of a greener future."[2] He believes in making an honest profit, but has no plans to patent the fuel, even after years of trial-and-error experimentation, in the hope that it can be made widely available and affordable. And his businesses employ as many women as men—including female

---

*Endnotes are grouped by chapter and begin on page 173.

mechanics—because of his commitment to gender equality. A modest man, Deamer does not make much of these practices. But framed as a set of principles, his approach to progress is decidedly cutting-edge: prosperity for Vanuatu should be environmentally resilient, broadly shared, and built on justice. Think of it as "progress-plus," a progress inspired by ethics.

The ethical dimension of Deamer's vision comes from his Bahá'í faith, his spiritual home for 41 years. One of the youngest of the world religions, with roots in mid-19th century Persia, the Bahá'í faith stresses the unity of the human family, gender and racial equality, and the complementary importance of science and faith, among other precepts.[3] And like many religions, it emphasizes service. "The desire to do something useful for the people around me is what drives my work," Deamer explains, adding that for him, service is another form of worship.[4]

Deamer is a single individual in an isolated corner of the world. But his life story embodies both a challenge and a hope for human advancement in the 21st century. The challenge is to redefine "progress:" to revamp economies and societies to work in harmony with the natural environment and serve all people. The hope is that religious communities and religious leaders worldwide will recognize—as many increasingly do—the powerful contributions they can make to this work and lend their considerable influence to it. Engaging the world's religions in an effort to re-imagine human societies can help ensure that the gains of the 20th century spread to all people into the indefinite future.

The Need for Inspired Progress

Despite the contributions of economic pioneers like Tony Deamer over the last 100 years, the word "progress" has fallen on hard times. Human activities are changing the Earth's climate, draining whole rivers, scalping forests, and unleashing a mass extinction—the first since the dinosaurs died off 65 million years ago.[5] The 20th century set records for organized violence, with more wartime deaths than in all previous centuries combined.[6] And its cornucopian abundance is as shameful as it is dazzling, given the billions in the human family who are left behind. These shortcomings are not just cranky footnotes to an otherwise stunning story of human achievement. Instead, they are major failures that threaten to unravel many of the great advances of the century.

A fundamental reassessment of the 20th century and a corresponding course correction are needed. Albert Einstein once noted that problems are not solved within the same mindset that created them, but require a fresh perspective. Indeed, the most important questions to guide a new vision of progress are not the "How" questions that fueled progress in the 20th century: how do we generate more revenue, more kilowatts, or more kilos per hectare, for example, although these remain important challenges.* More important are the elementary "What" questions: What is progress? What is the purpose of wealth? What is our proper relationship to other species, to other people, even to future generations? These questions were largely overlooked in the 20th century, or their answers were assumed to have been settled. But when widespread environmental and social dysfunctions—from a warming planet to a global obesity epidemic—threaten to remake whole societies for the worse, basic assumptions about progress demand a fresh look.

Progress as Bounded Creativity

A key argument of this book is that the impressive creativity of the 20th century lacked a strong set of ethical boundaries that could sustain progress over the long term and orient it toward prosperity for all. Human creativity was like a river without banks, the flow of innovation impressive but unchanneled. One missing riverbank was ecological wisdom, which might have helped us design human activities to work in step with nature. We built economies that were resource intensive, with an unprecedented toll on air, water, climate, and non-human species. The other absent bank was an ethic of human well-being, which might have helped rich and poor alike build more dignified and fulfilling lives. The poor suffer from persistent depri-

---

*Units of measure throughout this book are metric unless common usage dictates otherwise.

vation, while many prosperous people are afflicted by the corrosive effects of excess wealth. Without the guiding wisdoms of ecology and well-being—essentially Tony Deamer's vision, writ large—human cleverness has sown the seeds of economic and social disintegration.

The need for boundaries to guide human endeavors is a long-established tenet of human wisdom. Philosophers and spiritual leaders across cultures and throughout history have taught the importance of restraint, of channeling human energies within ethical boundaries. "Moderation in all things" is the oft-quoted wisdom of the Roman playwright Terence. Buddhist philosophy and Bahá'í teachings stress "the middle way," with excess and deprivation equally decried. And Mahatma Gandhi drew on his Hindu heritage to elaborate "seven deadly sins," blessings turned toxic by a lack of restraint:
- wealth without work
- pleasure without conscience
- science without humanity
- knowledge without character
- politics without principle
- commerce without morality
- worship without sacrifice.[7]

In sum, the world's civilizations have promoted restraint for centuries as a moral check on individual and societal excess.

Some thinkers go further, however, and argue that restraint is not merely a moral adornment to human activities, but a necessary ingredient for lasting progress. Thomas Berry, a Catholic priest and the author of several books that reflect on the meaning of the cosmos, argues that energy and the countervailing force of gravity—a cosmological expression of restraint—have been fundamental to creativity since the birth of our universe. The tremendous energy released during the Big Bang needed the constraining power of gravity, to shape matter into a productive universe.[8] Energy alone is diffuse and produces nothing, Berry notes, while discipline alone is rigid and lifeless. But in proper balance, the two can produce great creativity. For this reason, Berry argues, constraints, restraint, and boundaries are best understood as "liberating and energizing, rather than confining."[9] This wisdom is confirmed daily in small and great ways, from the child who masters the piano only with the discipline of regular practice, to resource-constrained countries like Japan that build more diversified and resilient economies than, say, many oil-rich nations do.

Of course, boundaries or limits are not ends in themselves: too tight a constraint can easily stifle progress. Totalitarian governments and rigidly planned economies in the 20th century extinguished the creativity that is vital to being human. Progress in those societies advanced like water in cement canals, whose flow is well bounded but unable to seek its own course. Natural rivers, by contrast, tend to be serpentine, carving out new paths even as they are contained by riverbanks. A major developmental challenge for human societies this century will be to encourage the creativity that drives human progress, while guiding that energy away from waste and self-destruction.

Making Progress Sustainable

An alternative approach to progress seeks to build on the impressive gains of the 20th century, but within boundaries established by ecology and the requirements of well-being. Known to many as "sustainable development," the concept has an implied ethical foundation: it promotes a vision of economies and societies that work in harmony with the natural environment and that extend the benefits of progress to struggling peoples everywhere. It acknowledges that the long term matters, and that our children and grandchildren have a moral claim on how decision makers today pursue progress. And it agrees that humans are more than economic beings, and that our progress, therefore, involves more than creating ever-greater levels of wealth.

Since its international debut in 1988, in a report called *Our Common Future* (also known as the Brundtland Report), sustainable development has slowly gained acceptance as a viable alternative to the 20th-century approach to progress. Defined as "development that meets the needs of the present without compromising the ability of future generations to meet their own needs," the concept was endorsed at the 1992 Earth Summit in Rio de Janeiro and re-affirmed at countless international gatherings since then.[10] And specific economic initiatives consistent with sustainable development—from the adoption of wind power to phasing out use of lead and mercury, to efforts to radically reduce waste in our cities—are being advanced by businesses, governments, and citizen activists everywhere. While hardly the norm in most countries, sustainable development nevertheless is becoming competitive as a vision for progress this century.

The World's Religions: Adding Value

But sustainable development arguably needs help. With each passing year, it becomes less and less likely that enlightened policies and greener technologies alone will be enough to build sustainable societies, as relentless and resource-intensive economic growth widens the gap between our impact on the planet and the impact it can endure. Framing the loss of forests and species not just as an environmental concern, but as a moral one, and describing gross inequality in a world of unprecedented wealth as a values issue, are powerful arguments that can supplement the new technologies and policies promoted by environmentalists and others interested in creating a sustainable brand of progress. As theologian Jay McDaniel has written regarding sustainability, we need "a transformation of mind and heart, desire and intention.... We need a sense of mystery and humility, gratitude and celebration. We need what some might call healthy religious wisdom."[11]

Indeed, the world's religions have many assets to lend to the effort to build sustainable progress, including moral authority, a long tradition of ethical teachings, and the sheer political power that comes from having so many adherents. In an era of extensive individualism, the community-centered concern of many religious traditions is especially valuable. Harvard biologist E. O. Wilson has noted that "organized religion is more concerned with the welfare of the group and with the collective good than any other institution" in most societies today.[12] Philosopher Max Oelschlaeger agrees that in western societies in particular, where individualism is highly valued, "Religious discourse...is perhaps the most promising way to expand our cultural conversation to include non-market values such as sustainability."[13] The ethical perspective of religion could help create the fresh outlook that Einstein regarded as necessary to deal with intractable problems.

But encouraging greater religious involvement in any societal project, especially one as broad-based as re-imagining progress, is a hard sell these days. With religious extremists making headlines around the globe, it's easy to wonder if religions are more a source of division and conflict than of peace and progress. Moreover, religious people and institutions, for the most part, have been slow to view the sustainability challenge as a religious concern. And some people argue that religions are too often part of mainstream thought and are unwilling to play the prophetic role that is a traditional religious strength. Religious writer and former monk Thomas Moore, for example, observes that religions often operate without challenging the dominant narratives of our time, including the narrative of progress.[14]

Such critiques are sobering. But it is also true that religious traditions are Phoenix-like, rising with renewed influence just when they are judged irrelevant, and often at times of societal desperation. Who would have imagined 15 years ago, for example, that evangelical Christians would be taking leadership positions on climate change, even pressing a president to change his position? Their renewed power and confidence comes from a reading of scripture through the lenses of a dying planet and a suffering human family. This process of reclaiming and reconstructing religious traditions, writes professor of religion Mary Evelyn Tucker, is critical if humans are to enjoy a century of inspired progress.[15] Today, with environmental and social crises emerging acutely across the globe, many congregations and religious leaders are re-discovering their own rich resources—from sacred writings to rituals and symbols—and tapping them to help address the plight of our planet and its people.

Grounded Idealism: The Approach of This Book

This book is an attempt to suggest some of the ingredients for a new understanding of progress. It operates at the level of principle, rather than nuts-and-bolts economic policy. In this big-picture role, it says little that the world's wisdom traditions haven't said for hundreds and even thousands of years. Yet its call for a bounded progress may be fresh in a world accustomed to full-throttle economic growth and open-ended individualism. And its appeal to religions to contribute their unique gifts in reshaping progress is a fresh expression of confidence in buffeted institutions that may doubt their relevance in modern societies.

The book is organized into four parts, each with a different look at progress. Part One considers the record of the 20th century, with an emphasis on the huge but often overlooked problems created by the century's many advances. Part Two argues that a new understanding of progress means rooting all economic activity in a healthy environment—which is, after all, the foundation for everything we do. Part Three proposes a new economic understanding of progress that stresses well-being, not just wealth, as an important goal of progress. And Part Four emphasizes the important role that ethics can play in advancing our understanding of progress. Each Part opens with an essay chapter discussing vision or worldview. The power of the modern worldview is considered in Part One, and elements of an alternative worldview are examined in Parts Two, Three, and Four.

The thoughts presented in this book, especially in the vision chapters that open the four Parts, are idealistic. But they are also realistic, and even timely, for several reasons. First, the global community may be more receptive than ever to the need for a new, sustainable kind of development. As deforestation, species loss, greenhouse gas emissions, and overuse of water continue apace, critical environmental thresholds are being crossed, and scientists from many disciplines tell us that major crises now loom before the human family. Meanwhile, the single-minded focus on wealth production is producing increasingly debilitating side-effects, such as obesity, that may cause people to question the current development track. Growing awareness of major global concerns may mean that human readiness to accept major changes in societal course is likely also growing.

Second, the book is realistic because most of the ideas presented here are already being implemented on at least a pilot basis. As a colleague at Worldwatch wryly noted in writing about the viability of renewable energy, "it is difficult to claim that something is impossible once it has already occurred."[16] Religious people and institutions worldwide are already spearheading pieces of a new vision of progress. While typically not part of mainstream religious agendas, these initiatives are gaining the support of religious leadership, and many are spreading quickly at the grassroots level. Given that the vast majority of the world's people subscribe to a religious tradition, the potential for these creative ideas to disseminate widely is huge.

Perhaps most importantly, this "idealistic" book is realistic because people, especially religious people, are often driven by vision. The visions vary, of course, but part of being a person of faith is having an idealism oriented toward creating a better world. Religious idealism has fueled societal change before. It helped gain independence for India from the world's foremost colonial power, and provided much of the driving energy in the U.S. civil rights movement and the movement to abolish apartheid in South Africa, to name just a few examples. Religion could play a transformative role once again this century, as part of the global struggle to give birth to a new and sustainable understanding of progress.

"Fundamental progress," wrote the great British philosopher Alfred North Whitehead, "has to do with the reinterpretation of basic ideas." The challenge today is to reinterpret progress itself, and to gear it toward service of people and societies within boundaries established by nature. Reframed this way, progress is likely to mean new advances in human well-being that build on or reshape the technological progress of the last century. The world's religious traditions, with their vast experience in the values that build lasting progress, can be invaluable teachers and allies in this effort.

"Smokey Mountain" dump in Manila, the Philippines

PART ONE

Progress Unraveling

CHAPTER 1

The Power of Vision: Worldviews Shape Progress

"What we do in the world flows from how we interpret the world."
—Charles Birch[1]

Worldviews are powerful, and shifts in them can be seismic. Consider what happened to Dave Bookless, a young British man on vacation with his wife Anne in 1990. The couple, lovers of natural beauty, chose to spend two weeks on the Isles of Scilly in the United Kingdom, where they marveled at the stunning seascapes, imposing cliffs, and unique wildlife. Dave and Anne were also committed Anglicans, and they took pleasure in reflecting during their vacation on verses from Genesis (the first book of the Hebrew scriptures and the Christian bible), in which God creates the seas and the land, plants and insects, animals and humans, with each day of creation culminating in the refrain, "And God saw that it was good." To Dave and Anne, Scilly was indeed very good.[2]

The islands, in the Atlantic Ocean southwest of Cornwall, are remote and rustic, and Dave and Anne had hauled in their provisions for the two weeks. As the days passed, Dave became aware of the refuse they were generating as they consumed food, paper towels, soap, and other items. By the end of their stay, he was astounded at the number of garbage bags he and Anne had filled. But the real shock came when he learned that the island had no provision for trash pickup: they, like other vacationers to Scilly, would have to dump their refuse over a cliff. For Dave, this was "a Damascus road experience," a reference to the religious conversion of Saul of Tarsus, the tormentor of early Christians who, while traveling to Damascus, was struck from his horse as a voice challenged him, "Saul, Saul, why do you persecute me?"[3]

Dave is a prayerful man, and he, too, sensed that God was speaking to him after he had tossed away his vacation rubbish. The voice—not audible, but deeply real to him nonetheless—was clear: "How do you think I feel about what you're doing to my world?" In that experience, Dave's view of reality and of his place in it changed forever, as a strong commitment to environmentalism flowered to complement his deep faith. He went on to become an Anglican priest, and his ministry has always included an environmental dimension. Today, he is executive director of the U.K. branch of A Rocha, a Christian conservation group operating in 15 countries worldwide.[4]

Dave's new orientation constituted nothing less than a shift in worldview—essentially, the assumptions people hold about the world and how it works, and one of the most influential determinants of one's priorities, politics, and lifestyle choices. Worldviews tell us what matters and what does not, what is more important and what is less so.[5] They are constructed from the answers we give to the greatest mysteries of our lives: Who am I? Why am I here? What is my relation to you and to the world around me? Often operating at a subconscious level, worldviews help people frame, sort, and accept or discard the barrage of data and information that comes at every human being every hour of the day.

Often, our worldview narrative is shared society-wide, with assumptions and beliefs that guide the collective life of whole peoples.[6] (See Sidebar 1–1.) Imagine Dave Bookless' experience being shared not just by his wife Anne, but by his entire hometown, or even by all Britons. And imagine that all were as deeply affected as Dave was. Such a shared experience might become a new thread in Britain's national narrative. All Britons might awaken to the amount of trash that they, individually and as a country, are generating. Throwing things away—a simple, daily act that most of us do reflexively—might become offensive, even sinful. A world without waste, perhaps never envisioned or dismissed as a utopian dream, might now become a

SIDEBAR 1–1. **Judeo-Christian Worldviews and the Environment**

A landmark 1967 essay by historian Lynn White asserted that the Judeo-Christian mandates to "subdue the Earth" and to "be fruitful and multiply" set the philosophical foundation for environmentally destructive industrial development in the West. The verses, he argued, created a worldview among Jews and Christians in which the natural world exists to serve humans.

The claim of Judeo-Christian culpability is controversial, however. It has been strongly criticized by many religious scholars, not least because White's argument is founded on just a few lines of scripture. Some critics of White note that a more complete reading of the Hebrew and Christian scriptures produces a much more nuanced understanding of the environmental perspective of these faith traditions. Others argue that even if White was on the mark, the evolving human understanding of sacred scriptures means that new interpretations of ancient verses—including environmental interpretations—are possible.

The critique of Judaism and Christianity, in turn, shaped the worldview of a generation of western environmentalists that religion is the problem, and that religious constituencies should be shunned in environmental work. But Sierra Club Executive Director Carl Pope sees this as a great mistake: Environmentalists have "made no more profound error than to misunderstand the mission of religion and the churches in preserving the Creation," Pope says. And he notes that White himself looked to religion for help, asserting that it would need to be part of the solution to the growing environmental crisis. Indeed, White ended the essay by suggesting that St. Francis of Assisi, the Tuscan lover of nature and the poor, become the patron saint of ecologists.

Source: See Endnote 6 for Chapter 1.

goal. Like the unseen rudder on a great ship, worldviews have the power to steer whole societies in new directions.

Building sustainable societies is not simply about changing policies and technologies, important as these are. Sustainability requires a new understanding our world and our place in it, a new appreciation of our relationship to nature and to a global community of human beings. It requires a different worldview.

The Modern Lens

Worldviews are shaped in part by the major challenges facing a country, community, or tribe. Historian of religions Huston Smith observes that human societies have faced three major kinds of societal challenges: obtaining food and shelter for survival (what he calls the nature problem); getting along with each other (the social problem), and relating to the universe at large (the religious problem). All three exist in any society, but their relative importance changes over time. Whether the nature, social, or religious problem dominates a group's outlook will affect how its people think about progress.[7]

The 20th century notion of progress was heavily shaped by the nature problem, and by our scientific response to it, which in turn emerged from the European Enlightenment of the 18th century. For Enlightenment thinkers, the world was like a machine: it was composed of interlocking parts that could be observed, analyzed, and even manipulated. Study the parts and tinker with them using the scientific method (repeatable experiments that allow inquisitive people to test ideas about how things work), and the world becomes far more knowable—and controllable—than our ancestors had ever believed. The Enlightenment gave Europeans and, later, people virtually everywhere, a sense that they could master nature, a greatly liberating revelation after eons of human suffering at the hands of plagues, famines, earthquakes, cyclones, and other wildcards of nature.

This sense of mastery of the physical world has given science a privileged place in human affairs. Indeed, the 20th century German philosopher Rudolf Carnap once wrote that "there is no question whose answer is in principle unattainable by science."[8] Many policymakers have agreed. Indian Prime Minister Jawarhalal Nehru asserted in a speech in 1960, "It is science alone that can solve the problems of hunger and poverty, of insanitation and illiteracy.... The future belongs to science, and to those who make friends with science."[9]

This confidence articulated the optimism of the time: progress, it seemed, would be largely a scientific endeavor.

But the Enlightenment worldview shaped human life well beyond science. It also made major contributions to how humans relate to each other—Huston Smith's "social problem." Confucian scholar Tu Weiming, a constructive critic of the Enlightenment worldview, nevertheless gives it credit for spreading values of liberty, equality, dignity of the individual, privacy, representative government, and due process of law.[10] These, he observes, helped create the dominant institutions of our day, including industrial capitalism, market economies, democratic governance, mass communications, research universities, bureaucracy, and professional organizations. These values and institutions, combined with the scientific power of the Enlightenment worldview, made it "the most dynamic and transformative ideology in human history," Tu concludes.[11]

On the other hand, the Enlightenment's contributions to the religious problem—how we relate to the universe—were minimal and largely derivative of its scientific advances. For many thinkers in the past three centuries, the advances of science shrank the spiritual realm of human experience considerably, to the point that the German philosopher Friedrich Nietzsche could speak of the "death" of God. Religion continued to exist, of course, and great theologians and religious thinkers have emerged in the past three centuries. But because the human relationship with the universe appeared to be explainable as a set of mechanical interactions, spiritual questions seemed increasingly irrelevant for societies dominated by the Enlightenment view of science.

The scientific worldview of the Enlightenment remains the principle guiding light for most industrial societies. "We mark our progress and project our future largely according to the machines we make and the factual discoveries we total up," notes religious writer Thomas Moore. "Information, research, evidence, reliability—these are the measures of our intellectual life. Like our Enlightenment ancestors, we don't trust the reality of a thing unless we can kick it and measure it. We hope for a perfected world that we will fully understand and control."[12]

Casting Shadows over Enlightenment

But many people today question the power of mechanistic science to explain the world. Many also question the value of today's increasingly extreme expressions of individualism, consumerism, and other perversions of Enlightenment values. The growing uneasiness with some aspects of the Enlightenment worldview may be laying the groundwork for an alternative way of understanding the world.

Regarding scientific endeavors, the critique is not that science is prone to technical error, but that manipulating small pieces of a machine-like physical universe causes us to lose sight of the big picture, with serious consequences. Consider, for example, traditional and scientific views of nitrogen, an important plant nutrient. Farmers for millennia supplied nitrogen to plants by applying animal manure to soils. But in the 20th century, scientists learned to isolate the element from ammonia and manufacture fertilizer, which farmers could easily apply to soils in huge quantities. The scientific advance greatly increased the fertility of crops and was one of the reasons for the huge increase in food production in the 20th century.

But while nitrogen molecules are the same whether delivered via manure or in the form of chemical fertilizer, the method of delivery makes a difference. In manure, nitrogen is bound up with organic matter, which helps keep the nutrient from washing away. By contrast, fertilizer is typically applied loose to cropland and is free to wash into rivers, then oceans, where it contributes to the creation of "dead zones" of depleted oxygen where no fish can live. Some of the dead zones are huge—one at the mouth of the Mississippi is larger than the U.S. state of New Jersey—and are a major aquatic disruption worldwide, having doubled in number since 1990.[13]

The mistake with our use of fertilizer and a host of other technologies of modern science, notes Indian physicist and activist Vandana Shiva, is that we assume that understanding parts of a system, such as molecules of nitrogen, means that we understand the whole. Separability allows us to abstract knowledge from its original context, which oversimplifies our more dynamic understanding of how the world works.[14] And when economics is married to this reductionist scientific model, the consequences are profound: "…a forest is reduced to commercial wood, and wood is reduced to cellulose fibre for the pulp and paper industry," Shiva writes.[15] Economic productivity becomes an overriding value, even if it reduces a forest's capacity to circulate water through a bioregion, or its ability to provide for a diversity of other species. "In this way, reductionist science is at the root of the growing ecological crisis, because it entails a transformation of nature such that its organic processes…and regenerative capacities are destroyed," Shiva argues.[16]

Shiva and others contrast this predominant reductionist science with the science of traditional (indigenous) knowledge, which tends to be holistic in its approach. It is an organic, rather than mechanistic, understanding of nature, where "concepts of order and power were based on interconnectedness and reciprocity" rather than on separability and manipulability.[17] Traditional knowledge is competitive in terms of its capacity to produce robust science, notes Shiva, but its rules and mode of operating are entirely different from that of modern science.

Indeed, more and more observers are taking a new look at indigenous forms of knowledge and find that these have their own explanatory power—a power that is sometimes rooted in myth and in spiritual outlooks and practices. Carol Jorgensen, director of the office of Indian Affairs at the U.S. Environmental Protection Agency, notes that native peoples of the Americas carry an extensive and powerful base of knowledge of how the world works, which is passed from generation to generation in the form of stories. "This knowledge is vast, tested and peer-reviewed," she says, meaning that it is judged for its truthfulness over time by other members of the tribe. "The only difference from modern science is that it is passed down orally, rather than published," she says.[18] These knowledge systems are often viewed as superstitious beliefs by modern science, especially when they are represented in the form of ritual, myth, or other spiritually oriented practices.[19]

"Too Much of A Good Thing"

Meanwhile, some of the social values emerging from the Enlightenment have been transformed into handicaps, observes the Confucian scholar Tu Weiming. In modern societies flush with freedom and prosperity, he notes, progress has degenerated into inequality, reason into self-interest, and individualism into greed. His conclusions may be broadly shared. Australian public health researcher Richard Eckersley finds that surveyed Australians increasingly express concern about a lack of public spiritedness and an increase in greed in their country, and they blame "too much of a good thing"—too much consumption or individualism, or excessive dependence on markets for solutions to societal problems.[20] Economists and policymakers, for example, justify the yawning gap between CEO and worker pay because a market indifferent to ethics has determined what executives and wage employees are worth, no matter the impact on inequality. Advertisers seem to convert St. Thomas Aquinas' seven deadly sins—pride, envy, avarice, wrath, gluttony, sloth, and lust—into virtues. And people in general seem to confuse individualism with self-centeredness and instant gratification.

Changing Worldviews

Many of the elements of the Enlightenment heritage, which is now nearly global in its reach, will be needed to build sustainable societies. Clearly, science is indispensable. Feeding a world of nine billion people and providing them with dignified levels of health care, education, housing, transportation, and employment is inconceivable without the power of science and technology. And Enlightenment values of individualism and market economics are too important to just toss aside. But it may be time to rethink the Enlightenment worldview, as Dr. Tu argues, amending it so that it equips societies to deal effectively with modern environmental and social challenges.[21] Indeed, both modern science and our social and economic values will likely flourish best in the 21st century if they answer to a new and higher standard, a broadly agreed set of ethics.

Fortunately, worldviews can evolve, and when they do religion is often a stimulus. Cultural historian Thomas Berry sees religion—along with education, business, and government—as a major source of society-wide change in the world, while psychologists see religion as one of four key sources of individual behavior change. Think about the influence of religion in societal transformations of the last few decades. Archbishop Desmond Tutu and religious people from around the world helped frame apartheid in South Africa as a moral issue, and used investment policies and moral suasion to work for its peaceful overthrow. Religious groups heavily influenced the Jubilee 2000 initiative to reduce developing country debt, and in the process reframed global thinking about debt. Infant baby formula, the high-tech way to feed infants in the 1960s, was reframed as a source of infant malnutrition in the 1970s, thanks in large part to pressure from religious people.[22] The power of religion to tackle great moral issues is clear, and clearly applicable to the environmental and social crises of the 21st century.

The courage Dave Bookless showed in changing his worldview will need to be replicated across whole societies if a worldview supporting sustainability is to be created. Citizens and leaders will need to overturn many of the assumptions about how we live, from what constitutes a normal diet or a normal way to get to work, to how our communities deal with poverty. A successful revamping of our societal worldviews will create a new view of progress rooted in holism and relationship. In the process, we may wonder how we ever came to embrace some of the pillars of 20th century progress. The more questionable ones assert that:

- the sole purpose of an economy is to generate wealth
- collecting material goods is the major goal of life
- waste is inevitable in a prosperous society
- mass poverty, while regrettable, is an unavoidable part of life
- the environment is an afterthought to the economy
- species and ecosystems are valuable for economic and aesthetic reasons, but do not have innate value
- ethics plays a negligible role in defining progress.

Overturning all of these "truths" will be central to building sustainable societies. Most are also of great interest to faith traditions worldwide. The looming question is whether we can look at the world in imaginatively new ways that help us create genuine human progress for the 21st century.

CHAPTER 2

The Paradox of Progress in the 20th Century

°"The world has achieved brilliance without conscience.
Ours is a world of nuclear giants and ethical infants."
—Omar Bradley[1]

Back-to-back press releases in early 2005 neatly summarize the paradox of progress in the 20th century. In late February, the U.S. government's Centers for Disease Control and Prevention (CDC) announced that life expectancy in the United States had reached 77.6 years, a span of a few months longer than the record reached in 2003.[2] While a welcome development, the report was hardly news, given the routine increases in life expectancy that had characterized most of the 20th century.

A few weeks later, *The New England Journal of Medicine* released an article analyzing the role of obesity on lifespans.[3] It noted that obesity already robs Americans of between four and nine months of life, a drag on the advances in longevity that the CDC had trumpeted the previous month. But the real news was the projection that, for the first time in U.S. history, the health impact of obesity eventually will be great enough to reverse, not just slow, the steady lengthening of lifespans. Obesity in children, the authors argued, is essentially a time bomb that will affect not just the quality, but the duration, of many Americans' lives.

This projected reversal of fortunes is emblematic of the double-edged sword that is 20th century progress. On one hand, the last 100 years saw more increase in well-being for more people than any previous civilization would have dreamt possible. Gains in health, food availability, and lifespans were the most tangible and dramatic evidence of these successes. But advances in economic opportunity, in freedom, and in improving the lot of women and racial and ethnic minorities were also notable, and made the century a virtual nirvana for hundreds of millions of people compared to the challenges and hardships that characterized life throughout much of human history. It seems indisputable that the 20th century offered more people in more places a greater chance to fulfill their potential than in all previous human experience.[4] (See Sidebar 2–1.)

On the other hand, many of the century's advances came at great cost: the last 100 years were by far the most violent, most environmentally destructive, and most wealth-skewed on record. Government leaders, business people, and citizens wielded unprecedented military and economic power with little sense of restraint or other ethics-based guidance. As a result, much of the cream of 20th century progress now shows signs of spoiling. The morphing of cornucopian food production into a global obesity epidemic may be the least worrisome of these turnabouts. Slowly, a growing chorus of scientists, policymakers, and citizens now acknowledge that last century's development path cannot—biologically, geophysically, economically, or ethically—continue to be the guiding vision for progress in the 21st century.

A Century of Violence

Governments over the past century showed a particular skill in using humanity's mastery of science and its ingenious technological innovations for military purposes. Advances such as the airplane, automobile, and rocket were quickly adapted for military use. Military needs, in turn, often drove technological development, typically through the funding of research and development programs at selected universities and corporations. Operating in parallel to the militarization of societies was a fledgling peace movement, from the British and American pacifists of World War I to conscientious objectors in Vietnam. But these movements were typically isolated and often lacked broad public support. Missing was a strong chorus of ethical voices

SIDEBAR 2–1. **Drivers of Progress in the 20th Century**

Rapid societal development in the last century can be credited to progress in overcoming three longstanding obstacles: low-grade sources of energy, a limited inventory of economically useful materials, and a modest base of scientific knowledge.

Consider energy. In the late 1600s, nearly 60 percent of all energy used in Europe came from horses and oxen and 25 percent came from wood—sources that pack far less energy than the coal, oil, and gas that fueled 20th-century machinery. And fossil fuels were highly versatile; their liquid forms, for example, made automobile and air travel possible. These advantages, along with the apparent abundance of the fuels, caused energy consumption to gallop ahead. Liberated from severe energy constraints, more work could be done by fewer people than ever before.

Materials were revolutionized as well. Earlier societies were built largely using wood, ceramics, and metals, along with cotton, wool, and leather. But today's economies use tens of thousands of materials that draw from all 92 naturally occurring elements in the periodic table. Advances in metals, polymers, ceramics, and composites were ongoing in industrial societies in the 20th century. Recall that plastics and aluminum, versatile materials that are ubiquitous in industrial societies today, were virtually unknown before World War I. Revolutionary as it has been, plastic is relatively simple compared to the myriad composites that have been developed in just the past decade. More materials with more desirable properties have meant more development options worldwide.

Perhaps the most impressive advance has come in the area of knowledge: whereas 10 scientific journals were published in the mid-1700s, some 20,000 exist today. New scientific disciplines proliferated as knowledge expanded: Columbia University in New York, for example, had 42 academic departments in 1900, but 85 by 2000. Increasing specialization pushed back the frontiers of knowledge and allowed scientists to explore the world of an increasingly dissected and parsed universe. This exploration, in turn, gave humans the capacity to manipulate the world around them to a remarkable degree.

In short, by pushing back the boundaries of energy, materials, and knowledge, humans have increased in number and complexity the combination of development options available to them.

Source: See Endnote 4 for Chapter 2.

that could offer a viable alternative to the logic of ever-more-powerful arms. Models of alternative approaches existed—Mahatma Gandhi helped India gain independence through a strategy of non-violence, and Martin Luther King used the same tactics to gain civil freedoms for blacks in the United States. But it was also clear that such work is slow and difficult, and the mobilizers to lead such efforts were rare across the century.

Just how violent the 20th century was is best appreciated from a long historical perspective, which researcher Michael Renner lays out nicely in *Ending Violent Conflict*, a paper from the Worldwatch Institute. Estimates of war deaths going back to the 1st century on the western calendar show a steady increase over time and a sharp upturn once the technologies and factories of the Industrial Revolution allowed political leaders to develop ever-more-lethal armies. War-related deaths in the 20th century were more than three times greater than in all previous centuries combined, back to the birth of Christ. Even after factoring in the much greater 20th century population (more people alive meant more could be killed), deaths in the 20th century were more than double the level of the 19th.[5] (See Table 2–1.) Clearly, human beings had developed a heightened capacity to wage war, and we used it.

Organized killing was of such a different magnitude that societies found new language to describe it, Renner observes. The mass elimination of Armenians, Jews, and Cambodians gave rise to the term *genocide*, for example. And the idea that American and Soviet governments possessed enough nuclear weapons to launch devastating attacks—then launch some more to "make the rubble bounce"—gave rise to the term *overkill*.[6] Our language, a measure of our consciousness, suggests that humanity was increasingly aware of its propensity for large-scale violence.

The unprecedented war deaths were the product of highly sophisticated levels of weapons development and organization for war.

TABLE 2–1. **War-Related Deaths over the Centuries**

Century	War Deaths (million)	Deaths per 1,000 People
1st to 15th	3.7	n.a.
16th	1.6	3.2
17th	6.1	11.2
18th	7.0	9.7
19th	19.4	16.2
20th	136.0	35.0

Source: See Endnote 5 for Chapter 2.

Emerging technologies were rapidly adapted for military use: in World War I some 206,000 airplanes, still a very young technology, were bought by the armies of the combatant nations. And longstanding military technologies were produced in far greater numbers than ever: France alone was producing 200,000 rounds of artillery *per day* during the war, compared with the 1,500 rounds that Napoleon used to defeat Prussia at the battle of Jena a century earlier. The military draft, an innovation of the 19th century that was in place in many countries by the start of the 20th, allowed for mass mobilizations: some 14 percent of Europe's population was sent to fight in World War I, compared with just 1 percent during the Napoleonic wars a little more than a century earlier.[7]

Yet World War I was only the opening act of the century's extensive violence. With World War II came adoption of the concept of total war—involving attacks not only on an opposing military, but against the enemy's economic targets, and even against civilian populations.[8] Casualties, therefore, were more than twice those of World War I. And large shares of national populations perished on the battlefield: the Soviet Union, Poland, and Yugoslavia lost 10–20 percent of their people; Germany, Italy, Japan, and China lost 4–6 percent; and Great Britain, France, and the United States lost about 1 percent.[9]

The rest of the century, while not posting any war with greater casualties than World War II, nevertheless saw a steady increase in the capacity of several militaries to do massive damage, primarily through the development of nuclear, biological, and chemical weapons, and other tools of mass destruction. And even beyond the activity of the superpowers, the human capacity for killing was revealed in shocking ways. The murderous rampage in Rwanda in 1994 saw more than 800,000 people killed within a three-month period.[10]

The capacity to wage war on a massive scale was a perversion of humanity's growing skill at scientific and technological development. That this perversion poses a major threat to human progress is obvious: a nuclear war between the United States and the Soviet Union and their allies would likely have set back human advance by centuries, and not just for two principal enemies. Even with the end of the Cold War, the threat of nuclear war between India and Pakistan, the possibility that terrorists might obtain "loose nukes" or biological or chemical weapons, and the possibility that the huge U.S. arsenal could be directed at a new strategic enemy remain as major threats to human advance in much of the world.

Environmental Abuse

Military innovations, especially the atomic bomb, demonstrated humanity's capacity to wield intense, episodic power. But environmental degradation over the 20th century signals a more subtle form of human power: the daily flexing of economic muscle in a way that grinds away at global resources. This power is arguably on a par with military weaponry: human economic activities are warming the planet, weakening the web of life, spreading toxins to remote regions, and creating imbalances in the natural cycles of water, carbon, and nitrogen. Never have human beings been able to affect the entire planet so dramatically. Where our species once regarded itself largely as a victim of nature, today we increasingly manipulate the natural world. So great is human alteration of the planet that we have created "Earth 2," in the words of environmental writer Bill McKibben.[11] But the new version is hardly improved, and in fact appears to be less able to support stable human economies.[12] (See Table 2–2, pp. 30–31.) Humanity's economic power, it seems, has become a threat to human progress.

But while humans increasingly dominate nature, we have proven to be very poor managers of natural systems. That's the conclusion of the Millennium Ecosystem Assessment (MA), a four-year global study commissioned by the United Nations that demonstrates that human activities since 1950 have altered ecosystems worldwide more extensively than at any time in human history. For example, more than half the total areas of six major terrestrial biomes (major environmental areas, such as forests and grasslands) have been converted by human activities, primarily to agriculture. The result has been a "substantial and largely irreversible loss in the diversity of life on Earth," according to the report. It projects that damage to ecosystems is likely to grow significantly in the first half of the 21st century. And it asserts that while reversing the damage is possible to some degree, this would require "significant changes in policies, institutions, and practices that are not currently underway."[13]

The study determined that 60 percent of the major services that the natural environment provides to human economies are being damaged or overused. Nature's capacity to provide resources such as wood or water, for example, is being stressed as human activities cut down forests and drain rivers and aquifers. Its ability to regulate floods and the climate, or to purify water, is also stressed in many regions. Supporting services, as when natural systems balance the amount of nitrogen found in land, sea, and air, are compromised when fertilizer use overloads rivers and oceans with nitrogen. "In effect, the benefits reaped from our engineering of the planet have been achieved by running down natural capital assets," says the report.[14]

Many of the changes to ecosystems are increasing the likelihood of "environmental surprise"—those accelerated, abrupt, and potentially irreversible disruptions that reduce the resilience of an ecosystem. Collapse of the cod fisheries off of Newfoundland is an example—catch plummeted from more than 800,000 tons annually to fewer than 200,000 tons in under a decade because of over-

TABLE 2–2. Indicators of Environmental Decline

Species

Biologists believe we are living amid the first major mass extinction since the one that killed off the dinosaurs 65 million years ago, a process that essentially unravels the biological work of billions of years in the blink of an eye. It is only the sixth mass extinction in our planet's 4.6 billion year history, and the first caused by human activities. Biologists estimate that species are going extinct at 100 to 1,000 times the natural rate; some 10–30 percent of all mammal, bird, and amphibian species are now threatened with extinction. Populations of some 1,000 vertebrates have declined by 40 percent since 1970.

Climate

Average global temperatures increased by about 1 degree Fahrenheit in the 20th century, and the planet continues to warm, with six of the warmest years since recordkeeping began in 1880 occurring since 1998. A United Nations panel of more than 1,000 scientists formed in 1988 declared that human activities are at least partially responsible for the rise. The most damaging activities are the combustion of oil and gas in factories, homes, and automobiles, which releases carbon dioxide, a greenhouse gas, and deforestation, which eliminates the carbon storage service provided by trees and releases carbon dioxide when forests are burned. Despite growing awareness of the dangers of greenhouse gases, emissions were 20 percent greater in 2005 than in 1990.

Forests

Earth has just over half of the pristine forested area it had 8,000 years ago. Most of the loss of forests globally occurred in the 20th century, and most of that came in the second half

---

fishing. The unexpected appearance of invasive species, such as the water hyacinth that spread from South America into Lake Victoria in East Africa is another example; it has damaged fisheries, lake transport, and hydropower generation in just a few years.[15] Surprises like these will continue to pop up simply because our understanding of

TABLE 2–2. CONTINUED

of the century. Unsustainable levels of logging continue, most notably in Southeast Asia, Russia, and Brazil—the Amazon lost an area the size of Belgium in 2004. Tropical rainforests are home to more species diversity than any other biomes in the world, making their loss especially critical. Forests are also critical for regulating rainfall and for water retention in soils, and they are frequently home to indigenous cultures.

Water
Major world rivers, including the Yellow, Colorado, Indus, and Nile, discharge little or no water to the sea for extended periods because of heavy withdrawals upstream. Meanwhile, groundwater in major agricultural regions of the United States, China, India, North Africa, and the Middle East are being overpumped faster than they are recharged by rainfall, threatening agricultural productivity in those regions. Over the past 50 years, two large dams (15 meters or higher) have been constructed somewhere on the planet every day on average; 3–6 times as much water is now held in reservoirs as in natural rivers. A 1996 study determined that human activities were already claiming 54 percent of the global accessible supply of fresh water.

Oceans
The Food and Agriculture Organization of the United Nations reported in 2005 that 24 percent of fish stocks globally are overexploited or depleted, and another 52 percent are fully exploited. The Australian government reports that 20 percent of the world's coral reefs—second only to tropical forests in biodiversity—are now damaged beyond recovery and another 24 percent face "imminent collapse," all because of human activities.

Source: See Endnote 12 for Chapter 3.

how ecosystems function is so poor. And future surprises could be truly calamitous. Scientists now worry, for example, that the Gulf Stream, which provides Northern Europe with a temperate climate, could be shut down by melting Arctic polar ice, leaving Europe in far more frigid conditions than it enjoys today.[16]

An innovative analytical tool known as the "ecological footprint" bolsters the MA argument that human activities are more than the planet can bear. Developed in the 1990s, the tool offers a measure of environmental impact by expressing, in units of land, an individual or society's use of nature's resources as well as nature's waste absorption capacity. For example, the hectares of forest needed to supply the wood in my home and the paper at my office, the farmland needed to grow my food, the vegetated area needed to absorb the carbon dioxide from my car and from the power plant that heats my home—this total land area is a measure of my ecological impact, or footprint, on the Earth.* It turns out that the average person on the planet has a footprint of 2.2 hectares.[17]

The tool also tracks Earth's capacity to supply our demands, a measure called "ecological capacity." There are some 1.8 hectares of ecological capacity—biologically productive land—available for every person on the planet. Note the imbalance: with 2.2 hectares of demand and 1.8 of supply, the average person is using about 0.4 hectares more than the planet can provide, an overshoot of 22 percent. The tool makes clear that humanity is collectively living larger than the planet can support.[18] (See Table 2–3).

Living large is possible—for a while—by tapping nature's "savings accounts." When we cut down forests faster than nature can regenerate them, or pump from wells or reservoirs faster than nature can replenish them, we dip into the planet's resource reserves. These reserves have long been useful in helping societies survive lean times—as when a well supplies water during a prolonged drought. But 20th century economies began to rely on these reserves not as insurance but to supply ongoing needs. This imprudent behavior can go on for a few years or a few decades, depending on the resource being depleted. But these reserves are finite and will eventually be rendered unusable.

---

*The ecological footprint is inherently conservative as a measure of environmental impact. It does not measure toxic waste or species extinctions (since no amount of land area can sustainably support toxics or replace extinct species), and it measures the environmental impact of water use only indirectly.

TABLE 2–3. **Footprint and Ecological Capacity of Selected Country Groupings, 2002**

Country or Region	Footprint per Person	Ecological Capacity per Person	Overshoot
	(hectares)	(hectares)	(percent)
High-income countries	6.4	3.4	88
Middle-income countries	1.9	2.1	—
Low-income countries	0.8	0.7	14
World	2.2	1.8	22
Selected countries			
United States	9.7	4.7	106
EU-25 + Switzerland	4.7	2.3	104
China	1.6	0.8	100

Source: See Endnote 18 for Chapter 3.

Human overexploitation of the planet can be illustrated by graphing the world ecological footprint against Earth"s ecological capacity.[19] (See Figure 2–1, p. 34.) Earth's ecological capacity is largely fixed (the slight rise in the graph reflects an increase in the productivity of agricultural land), but the world ecological footprint has continued mostly upward. In the mid-1980s, according to the Global Footprint Network, the lines crossed, meaning that the human family as a whole started to live beyond its means. (Overshoot at local levels had been occurring for decades, but in the 1980s the problem became a global one.) The more the footprint line rises above the ecological capacity line, the more traumatic the reckoning will likely be when reserves are depleted.

Ethical voices against the ongoing degradation of the environment were uncommon in the first half of the 20th century, with early conservationists such as John Muir and visionaries like Aldo Leopold being standout exceptions. The strongest voices in the United States have emerged since 1962, when Rachel Carson published *Silent Spring*, a critique of the standard path of progress. Successes came quickly, with Earth Day and new environmental laws in place by the 1970s. While the environmental movement had more victories more quickly than the peace movement, only in the 1990s

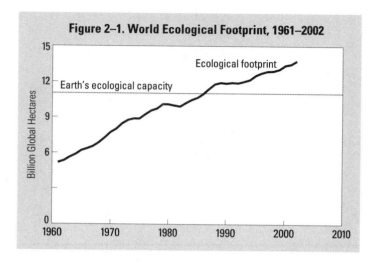

Figure 2–1. World Ecological Footprint, 1961–2002

did it begin to articulate a critique of the reigning resource-intensive economic model of progress. The foundation laid at the close of the 20th century is a good one. But the fact that virtually every global environmental trend of importance continues to worsen suggests that voices on behalf of the environment will need to be stronger still.

Poverty Amid Fabulous Wealth

A third major disappointment in the use of human power in the 20th century was the failure of societies to eliminate mass poverty. Such a goal may seem unreasonable: poverty, after all, has been a constant in most urbanized societies for the thousands of years that societies have existed. Yet the sheer magnitude of wealth generated in the 20th century made the elimination of at least the most severe deprivation an achievable goal globally for the first time in recorded history. That this did not happen, therefore, arguably stands as one of the greatest moral failings of humankind in the 20th century.

Global economic output, which hovered at around $100 billion (in constant 1990 international dollars) from the 1st century through the year 1000, rose steadily thereafter and rapidly with the Indus-

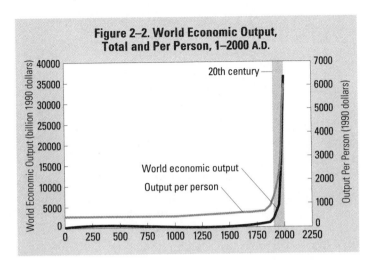

Figure 2-2. World Economic Output, Total and Per Person, 1–2000 A.D.

trial Revolution, crossing the trillion-dollar mark by the middle of the 19th century.[20]* (See Figure 2–2.) But in the 20th century, economic growth was truly explosive: an 18-fold increase in output between 1900 and 2000 brought gross world product from $1.97 trillion to $36.6 trillion. The surge was huge even after taking population growth into account. Wealth generated globally per person grew nearly fivefold, from $1,262 in 1900 to $6,045 in 2000. No previous generations in human history had ever seen anything like this vast increase in economic output.

This wealth, however, was distributed highly unevenly. The World Bank noted in 1995 that between 1820 and 1992, "while the world got richer, income inequality—relative and absolute, international and global—increased tremendously."[21] A few numbers paint the picture of modern inequality:

- In 1960, gross domestic product per person in the world's 20 richest countries was 18 times greater than in the poorest 20; by 1995, that the gap had grown to 37 times.[22]
- In the United States in 2001, average CEO compensation was

---

*Unless otherwise noted, all dollar figures are in U.S. dollars.

$11 million, some 350 times greater than the pay of the average factory worker—and the gap increased a stunning fivefold in a single decade, between 1990 and 2001.[23]

- In 1998, the United Nations Development Programme reported that the world's richest three *individuals* had assets equal in value to the combined GDPs of the world's 48 poorest nations.[24]

The reality on the ground was sobering. At the end of a century of unprecedented wealth creation, some 1.1 billion people—more than 1 in 6 worldwide—did not have access to safe drinking water, while 842 million—nearly 1 in 7—were classified by the U.N. Food and Agriculture Organization as "chronically hungry," a number that was on the rise again after several years of modest decline.[25] Meanwhile, infant mortality in low-income countries in 2000 was some 13 times greater than in high-income countries.[26]

At the same time, people in wealthy countries enjoyed cornucopian consumer choices, from daily indulgences such as candy and soda to major purchases like ocean cruises and sports cars. And consumption in wealthy countries implies disproportionate claims on the world's resources. The United States alone, with less than 5 percent of the global population, used about a quarter of the world's fossil fuel resources—burning up nearly 25 percent of the coal, 26 percent of the oil, and 27 percent of the world's natural gas in 2000.[27]

Add consumption by other wealthy nations, and the dominance of just a few countries in global materials such as metals is clear. The United States, Canada, Australia, Japan, and Western Europe—with among them 15 percent of the world's population—consumed 61 percent of the aluminum produced in 2001, 60 percent of the lead, 59 percent of copper, and 49 percent of steel.[28] Poorer nations consume at entirely different levels: the average American used 22 kilograms of aluminum annually at the turn of the century, while the average Indian used 2 kilos and the average African, less than 1 kilo.[29] Disparities in resource use are also apparent through ecological footprint analysis. The footprint for each Bangladeshi in 2000 stood at just 0.5 hectares, compared with more than 9.5 hectares for the average American.[30]

Coming Soon: A Global Reckoning

Ever-more-deadly weapons, environmental decline, gross inequalities—where is it all headed? The outlook is sobering. On the military side, the number of wars and related deaths has dropped since the end of the Cold War, but the larger forces that make war possible—the development of armaments and the mobilization of large sectors of society for war—are still in place. And people today must grapple with the distressing historical fact that weapons, once produced, eventually get used. Without strong frameworks of ethics to guide the way we think about security—political mechanisms for international collaboration and conflict resolution—tit-for-tat buildups of more powerful arms will surely remain the strategy nations use to try to increase their security.

Regarding inequality, there is a modicum of good news. The rapid increase in incomes in the two most populous countries, China and India, appears to be dampening global income inequality somewhat, though even this is disputed by analysts.[31] And whether such growth can be sustained remains to be seen. China, for example, has seen a large increase in civil unrest in recent years, from 8,700 protest incidents in 1993 to 74,000 in 2004, as economic inequality *within* the country has grown.[32] And to the extent that Chinese and Indian successes simply help push the world as a whole to greater levels of unsustainability, as measured, for example, by an expanding global ecological footprint, economic success there could well be tenuous.

Indeed, environmental decline may be the greatest challenge facing the human family. Perhaps the best long-term analysis of human prospects on an increasingly unhealthy planet is the World 3 computer model, which looks at humanity's environmental and social future. First run in the early 1970s and explicated in the book *The Limits to Growth*, the model warned that the world was headed for economic collapse within a few decades because of environmental abuse and resource depletion. The decline is gradual at first: for some time as the model is run, all is well as economies tap the planet's cornucopian resources to fuel robust growth. But then rather suddenly, "the underlying mechanisms that produced prosperity flip and collapse," says Dennis Meadows, one of the leaders of the modeling effort. Specifically, as societies need more water, land, and energy, their capital costs increase, making it more and more expensive to sustain industrial growth, and even to provide basic needs. Soon, resource-intensive industrial societies can no longer function. Meadows sees this dynamic unfolding today in the negative economic growth per person registered by nearly one-third of the world's countries throughout the 1990s.[33]

Meadows has rerun the model twice since its 1970s debut, most recently in 2003. Each time, it produces the same general result: resources are overdrawn and the environment is degraded until a global economic collapse occurs, sometime in the mid-21st century. But the options that allow us to avoid collapse have become fewer each time the model is run. In a 2005 interview, Meadows explained it this way:

> What we find over and over again for the last three decades is that as long as you have exponential growth in population and industry, as long as those two embedded growth processes are churning away to produce larger and larger demands on the base, it doesn't make any difference what you assume about technology, about resources, about productivity. Eventually you reach the limits, overshoot and collapse.... Even if you make heroic assumptions about technology and resources it only postpones collapse by a decade or so. It's getting harder and harder to imagine a set of assumptions that allow the model to produce a sustainable result.[34]

When the interviewer asks Meadows what would convince him that societies have turned the corner and are headed in the right direction, his response is revealing. A scientist who has made his name in the abstract world of computer modeling, a man of algorithms and equations, Meadows nevertheless does not reach for a technical answer: "Of course energy efficiency and recycling waste...are important. But the real key indicators lie in the social values and cultural norms." Earlier in the interview he makes the same point: "What's needed in our model to produce a different result is a change in our underlying values, a change in attitudes about population, a change in preferences in consumption, a change in our attitude to the poor across the globe."[35]

Indeed, values and norms will likely become much more important if, as Meadows suggests, policymakers cannot rely on economic growth (of the resource-intensive kind) to reduce poverty.[36] This has been the policy prescription in many countries for decades: enlarge the economic pie in the hope that everyone, even the poorest, will eventually benefit. But if the pie is essentially fixed—if there are limits to resource-intensive growth—what tools are available to help governments deal with the political problem of disgruntled citizens who feel trapped in poverty? Technology is surely one of those tools, but technology will be hard-pressed to provide for a growing population within tightly constrained resource limits. A set of widely agreed norms—ethics—to guide the human family through challenging times could be a huge boost to peace and prosperity this century.

Addressing issues of war and peace, environmental decline, and inequality in the coming century will require a much greater dollop of ethics and spirituality from a much broader segment of societies than was the case last century. This century will require a new confidence on the part of the world's religions, a confidence rooted in the conviction that their contributions to a sustainable world are indispensable. Without ethics, without a deep spiritual respect for life and for the planet that supports us, progress over the next 50 years will likely be little more than progressive decline.

CHAPTER 3

Tools for Course Correction: Religions' Contributions

"Power based on love is a thousand times more effective
and permanent than power derived from fear."
—Mahatma Gandhi[1]

T he notion that religions might be influential enough to help shift whole societies onto new paths may seem fanciful. Religions typically lack armies, diplomatic prowess, control of legislatures, or other conventional sources of power that can shape a country's fundamental direction. But religious influence, often subtle and underestimated, can be astonishingly powerful. Consider the case of the Christmas Truce of 1914.[2]

German and British troops had dug into opposing trenches for months, facing each other across fields known as No Man's Land that were often less than 100 meters wide. Most had expected to be home by Christmas, because World War I, begun a few months earlier, was forecast to be short. Instead, they found themselves bogged down in a stalemate in December of the first year of the war, fighting cold, fatigue, and hunger in their trenches as much as they fought the enemy.

Then, on Christmas Eve, something extraordinary happened. By most accounts, it started on the German side: soldiers there began to sing "Stille Nacht" (Silent Night) and to put up Christmas trees outside their trenches. The British, recognizing the melody, gradually accompanied the German troops with the English version of the carol. The dynamic across the battlefield had a transformative effect. Soldiers began to shout entreaties to their enemies across the field, or to hoist signs saying, "we won't shoot, you won't shoot." Troops from each side slowly emerged from the trenches, met in No Man's Land, and began to fraternize with the men they had targeted for death just hours before. Many shared a soldier's luxuries—chocolate, cigarettes, or flasks of liquor—as signs of friendship and trust building. Others set up soccer matches in No Man's Land. At least for that night, and in some places along the front for several days, enemy combatants came together and World War I largely ground to a halt, trumped by a religious celebration.

Many non-religious explanations have been offered for this remarkable turn of events. A truce had been planned anyway for Christmas Day in order to bury the dead, so truce was already on the soldier's minds that Christmas Eve. The soldiers had expected to be home by Christmas, and were eager to celebrate. The trenches were sometimes within sight of villages—a sign of civilization that may have helped them preserve their own civility. But by most accounts (which are based on letters written by soldiers to their hometown newspapers), the soldiers' common identification with Christmas, and with symbols associated with it such as Christmas trees and Christmas carols, had a powerful impact on the men. Music and symbols, infused with deep meaning for combatants on both sides, proved more powerful than bullets, artillery, or even orders from generals to return to the trenches.[3]

It is possible to make too much of the Christmas Truce. After all, the event was not repeated in subsequent years of the war, and religious symbolism apparently played no role in stopping or even shortening the conflict. Whatever remarkable power religious identity held for the soldiers that Christmas Eve seems akin to a volcanic eruption or an earthquake—an immensely powerful force that is nevertheless difficult to predict, control, or sustain. Such a force may seem an unlikely tool for building sustainable societies in the 21st century.

But this conclusion may be too hasty, given the growing engagement of religious groups, motivated largely by their faith, on issues of sustainable development. Using their capacity to provide meaning, but other assets as well—their moral authority, sheer numerical presence in most societies, material assets such as property and investments, and capacity to build communities—the world's faith and indigenous traditions are engaging some of the most momentous issues of our age. If the world's faiths choose to embrace these issues in a comprehensive, large-scale way, they could give a distinctive spiritual and ethical stamp to progress in the 20th century—a stamp that may be indispensable to building sustainable societies.

The following sections describe five assets that religions bring to sustainable development efforts.

Asset #1: Meaning

Providing people with a sense of meaning and purpose is arguably one of the most powerful assets that religions wield, but it may also be the least appreciated. Having purpose and meaning is necessary for an individual's emotional and psychological health, and can spell the difference between tackling a set of goals each day and remaining disengaged from them. A sense of purpose can also unify an entire country around a national goal, whether it is collecting rubber and scrap metal for recycling in World War II, or doing the same for sustainable development in the 21st century.

Religious and indigenous traditions convey meaning in many ways, one of the most powerful of which is storytelling. Sacred texts are replete with stories whose power endures over millennia because their lessons resonate deeply, even as the social context changes markedly. Reverend Dave Bookless, for example, found environmental wisdom in his fresh reading of the Book of Genesis after his trash-disposal experience on the Isles of Scilly. A good example is the story of Noah's Ark, in which the biblical figure Noah herds the male and female of every living species onto an ark to protect them from a great flood. "It's about a huge environmental crisis, it's about climate change, it's about preventing species loss," Dave explains with great animation. "And the story shows that while God was in control, he required hard work of humans"—a parallel, Dave believes, to the responsibilities that people and societies carry today to preserve Creation.[4] Stories in general are a profoundly meaningful form of human communication. When coupled with the authority that religious teaching holds for many people, stories have the potential to changes lives or societies.

Faith and indigenous groups also convey meaning through the use of symbols and rituals, repeated patterns of activity that carry the often inexpressible meaning of human experience. Symbols and ritual communicate at a visceral level that is often beyond the capacity of language to convey. Thus, performing ablutions before prayer in the Bahá'í, Christian, Hindu, Jewish, Muslim, and other traditions is a non-rational but deeply meaningful form of communication for believers. Ritual and symbols are not exclusively religious tools, of course. A president or prime minister singing the national anthem at a sporting event, hand over heart, is engaging in a powerful ritualistic behavior that speaks deeply to compatriots. But religious people are particularly experienced and comfortable with ritual, in part because so much of religion is ineffable and beyond the capacity of language to convey.[5] (See Sidebar 3–1.)

Ritual communication arguably has a special place in the movement to create sustainable societies because it has long had the effect of protecting the natural environment. Cultural ecologist E. N. Anderson observes that among indigenous societies that have managed resources well for sustained periods, the credit often goes to "religious or ritual representation of resource management."[6] The Tsembaga people of New Guinea, for example, have elaborate pig festivals that include ritual slaughters and pig-eating rituals. These play a key role in maintaining ecological balance, in redistributing land and pigs among people, and in ensuring that the neediest are the first to receive limited supplies of pork.[7] The link between ritual and environmental protection, perhaps surprising to the western mind, is understandable in view of the fundamental importance—indeed the inseparability—of spirit and nature in many indigenous traditions.[8]

Such rituals, often dismissed as superstition by modern peoples, seem to have equipped indigenous people to be better environmental stewards than industrial societies are. The reason, says Anderson, is that environmentally oriented ritual helps people forge emotional connections with nature, creating a strong motivation to value and protect it. By contrast, ties to nature in industrial societies tend to be weak, because the specialized roles of our complex economies allow us to live without the need to grow our own food, fetch our own water,

SIDEBAR 3–1. Leveraging Nature for Religious Impact

Religious symbols are often enormously powerful in themselves, but their meaning can be magnified when they harness the power of non-religious symbolism. At Adat Shalom Reconstructionist Congregation in Bethesda, Maryland, for example, special thought went into the design of the *ner tamid*, the eternal light (traditionally an oil lamp) found in all synagogues that symbolizes God's eternal and immanent presence in the community and its members.

In most synagogues today, the ner tamid is fueled by gas or electricity. But the environmentally conscious Adat Shalom community saw great symbolic, and literal, power in the sun. They chose solar cells to power the lamp, and designed it to refract sunlight streaming into the synagogue from outside. They also designed the arm supporting the lamp to act as a sundial. As a result, the sunlight hits the ner tamid differently throughout the morning service, and the shadow it casts changes seasonally as the sun's placement in the sky changes.

The congregation's choices reflect not only members' "green" orientation, but their insight that the gifts of Creation could be used to enrich their weekly worship.

Source: See Endnote 5 for Chapter 3.

or cut our own fuel wood.[9] How many of us in industrial countries, for example, can accurately describe where our water comes from, how far the lettuce on our tables has traveled, or where our garbage and sewage winds up?

Today, a growing number of religious communities worldwide are finding room within traditional rituals for valuing the natural world and emphasizing other aspects of sustainability. One example is found in the eco-kosher movement in American Judaism. "Keeping kosher" is the ancient practice of observing dietary laws (such as not consuming meat and dairy products together) that have great symbolic and practical value for Jews. It is a practice that raises consciousness of the abundant generosity of the divine, and of humans' correct relationship to the fruits of God's creation. Some observant Jews are now asking what the kosher tradition might have to say about food and other consumables in an environmentally degraded world. They have developed the concept of eco-kashrut (eco-kosher): right-eating and right consumption to preserve environmental health.

Rabbi Goldie Milgram, executive director of Reclaiming Judaism as a Spiritual Practice, notes that three ancient Jewish *mitzvot*, or commandments, might help supply the rationale and parameters for keeping eco-kosher. *Bal Tashchit*, the injunction not to waste, could be invoked to turn Jewish consumers away from food packaging that is excessive or non-recycled. *Tzaar Baalei Chayyim*, the commandment to avoid cruelty to animals, might have special resonance in an age of large-scale livestock production, where animals are sometimes raised inhumanely. And *Shmirat Haguf*, the requirement that people take care of their bodies, might have particular relevance regarding foods that have been sprayed with pesticides.[10] The religious framing of otherwise commonplace ethical demands—don't waste, don't be cruel to animals, and take care of your body—gives new meaning and power to these exhortations, and could make them attractive to Jewish consumers.

Another example of the application of ritual to sustainability comes from Thailand, where "environmentalist monks" advocate for conservation and social justice within a Buddhist framework. One example of the monks' success comes from the Thai village of Giew Muang, where in 1991 a monk named Prhaku Pitak helped breathe new life into a local forest conservation movement that had been ineffective in combating forest degradation. Pitak's educational work with the villagers invoked their Buddhist heritage: he dubbed the Buddha "the first environmentalist" because of the importance of trees in the Buddha's life. And he stressed the interrelatedness of trees, water supply, and food production, capitalizing on the Buddhist teaching of "dependent origination," the interdependence of all things.[11]

Pitak also understood the power of ritual and used it to make links between villagers' spirituality and forest conservation. Many of the villagers were animists as well as Buddhists, so Pitak followed their suggestion to enlist a village elder in asking the village's guardian spirit to bless the conservation effort. A shrine was built to the spirit, and offerings were made from every household in the village. Then Pitak turned to Buddhist rituals. Joined by 10 other monks and surrounded by the villagers, Pitak "ordained" the largest tree in the forest, wrapping a saffron robe around it and following most of the rite used in a normal ordination ceremony. This symbolic act communicated to the entire village that the forest conservation effort was not merely a civic activity, but was imbued with sacred meaning. Villagers were united in seeing the trees not just as resources, but as part of a larger ecological and mystical reality, which placed them in a millennia-long chain of humanity that has used ritual to help maintain sustainable resource use.

While rituals and other aspects of religious practice have been modified regularly over the centuries to help religious communities address contemporary challenges, ritual adaptation is sensitive: adapted rituals run the risk of being manipulated cynically for political or other purposes. Conscious of this, the environmentally sensitive Adat Shalom congregation in Maryland used many of the aspects of eco-kashrut to govern the way they purchase and use food at the synagogue. But they did not call it "keeping eco-kosher" per se. Sensitive to the millennia-old Jewish tradition of keeping kosher, some congregation members were concerned that changes to it might diminish its historical significance. Indeed, ritual is a deep form of communication, and changes that appear to tamper with its many layers of significance are likely to be resisted by believers. On the other hand, to the extent that faith groups find the environmental and social aspects of sustainable development to be issues of genuine religious concern, the use of ritual and symbol to convey the importance of these issues may come naturally over time.[12]

Asset #2: Moral Capital

Beyond religions' capacity to provide meaning for people's lives lies a second asset: their ability to inspire and to project moral authority. While hardly omnipotent in imposing their views, religious leaders often have the ear of their congregations, and major leaders such as the Dalai Lama, the Archbishop of Canterbury, the Ecumenical Patriarch, or the Pope often get broad media coverage—no small advantage in the modern cacophonous media environment.

Moral authority, like the capacity to help people find meaning in life, is an intangible asset and for that reason often overlooked or downplayed. Asked in 1935 if the Pope might prove to be an ally of the Soviet Union, Communist leader Josef Stalin is said to have replied scornfully, "The Pope? How many divisions has he got?" The dictator's response betrays a dim understanding of the power that accrues to persons and organizations that appeal successfully to the depths of the human spirit. Indeed, papal influence exercised through the Solidarity protest movement in Poland in the early 1980s was an important factor in the eventual unraveling of Communist rule in Eastern Europe. Similarly, the Dalai Lama strongly affects Chinese government policy toward Tibet, even though he has lived in exile since 1959. Charisma and moral suasion are not the exclusive reserve of religious leaders, of course, but the role of these leaders in interpreting religious teaching—often teachings with strong moral content—gives them a particular moral authority when they speak out.[13]

Yet the power of moral authority to help build a sustainable civilization arguably falls far short of the potential. Consider the question of going to war in Iraq. In 2002, the heads of 48 U.S. Protestant and Orthodox denominations and religious orders—including the head of the Council of Bishops of the United Methodist Church (the denomination of U.S. President George W. Bush)—wrote to the president voicing their opposition to war.[14] Pope John Paul II publicly expressed opposition, dispatching an envoy to deliver the message directly to the president.[15] And the National Council of Churches issued its own official statement of opposition.[16] Despite the public entreaties, a survey by The Pew Research Center for the People and the Press just before the United States invaded found that solid majorities of Catholic and Protestant Americans supported a war. It also found that religious beliefs were influential in shaping the war views of only 17 percent of those who regularly attend religious services.[17]

The tepid response to religious leaders' calls can arguably be explained by *insufficient* leadership on the war issue, especially by local clergy. Some 78 percent of those surveyed said that their minister, priest, or rabbi had not mentioned the war in sermons, or had referred to it without taking a position. Only 3 percent reported hearing preaching against the war—and 15 percent heard sermons in support of the war. Many of the faithful expected more of their leaders: nearly a third of respondents thought that religious leaders were saying too little on the war, while only 15 percent thought that leaders had spoken out too much.

More consistent religious leadership might have made a difference in the public response to the president's call to arms. In contrast to their views on Iraq, those surveyed said that religion strongly influences their positions on social issues such as abortion, the death penalty, or gay marriage, topics that often get ongoing attention from religious leaders. Consistent religious leadership, it seems, can sway public opinion. The open question is whether religious leaders will spend their moral capital on the environmental, social, and peace questions that constitute some of the great societal questions of our day.

Asset #3: Numbers of Adherents

Turning to the more worldly religious assets, a third source of power for religions is the sheer number of followers they claim. Although the data are estimates, roughly 85 percent of people on the planet belong to one of 10,000 or so religions, and 150 or so of these faith traditions have at least a million followers each. Adherents of the three largest traditions—Christianity, Islam, and Hinduism—account for about two-thirds of the global population today. Another 20 percent of the world's people subscribe to the remaining religions, and about 16 percent are non-religious.[18] (See Table 3–1, p. 50.)

Degrees of adherence among the billions of religious people vary greatly, of course, as does the readiness of adherents to translate their faith into political action or lifestyle choices. And many believers within the same religion or denomination may interpret their faith in conflicting ways, leading them to act at cross-purposes. But the raw numbers are so impressive that mobilizing even a fraction of adherents to the cause of building a just and environmentally healthy society could advance the sustainability agenda dramatically. Adding

TABLE 3–1. Major Religions: Number of Adherents and
Share of Global Population, 2005

Religion	Adherents	Share of World Population
	(million)	(percent)
Christianity	2,001	31.3
Islam	1,300	20.3
Hinduism	900	14.1
Confucianism and Chinese Folk Religion	394	6.2
Buddhism	376	5.9
Indigenous Religions	300	4.7
African Traditional and Diasporic	100	1.6
Sikhism	23	0.4
Juche	19	0.3
Spiritism	15	0.2
Judaism	14	0.2
Bahá'í Faith	7	0.1
Jainism	4	0.1
Shintoism	4	0.1
Cao-Dai	4	0.1
Zoroastrianism	3	0.0
Total	5,464	85.4

Source: See Endnote 18 for Chapter 3.

non-religious but spiritually oriented people to the total boosts the potential for influence even more.

Influence stemming from having a large number of followers is further enhanced by the geographic concentration of many religions, which increases their ability to make mass appeals and coordinate action. In 120 countries, for example, Christians form the majority of the population. Muslims are the majority in 45 countries, and Buddhists are in 10.[19] When most people in a society have similar worldviews, leaders can make mass appeals using a single, values-laden language. Pakistan did this in 2001 when, as a result of its National Conservation Strategy, the government enlisted Muslim clergy in the

North West Frontier Province to launch an environmental awareness campaign based on teachings from the Qu'ran. Government leaders and nongovernmental organizations (NGOs) saw the religious leaders as a critical part of the campaign, given their broad presence in the country and the fact that in some regions more people go to mosques than to schools.[20]

Of course, size is not always the most important determinant of the potential to help shape a sustainable world. Indigenous traditions, typically small in number, often possess great wisdom on how to live in harmony with nature. Most have an intimate knowledge of their local bioregion, which in turn is the source of revelation, ritual, and collective memory for them. And their worldviews tend to integrate the temporal and spiritual realms. Although the stereotype of indigenous people as good stewards of their resource base may be overstated, specialists in religion and ecology see indigenous cultures as having rituals of reciprocity and respect for nature that enable them to leave an especially small environmental impact. These characteristics give them particular moral relevance that can be an important source of knowledge and inspiration in building a sustainable world.[21]

In some countries, the broad base of adherents is receptive, if not yet committed, to issues of sustainability, which further increases religions' potential contribution to building a sustainable world. In a survey of Americans by The Biodiversity Project in Wisconsin, for example, 56 percent of respondents said that environmental protection is important because the Earth is "God's creation."[22] And the religiosity of a broad swath of the American public led the Sierra Club in 2002 to collaborate with the National Council of Churches on television ads against drilling in the Arctic National Wildlife Refuge.

Asset #4: Land and Other Physical Assets

The fourth asset that many religions can bring to the effort to build a sustainable world is substantial physical and financial resources. Real estate holdings alone are impressive. The Alliance of Religions and Conservation, an NGO based in the United Kingdom, estimates that religions own up to 7 percent of the land area of many countries.[23] And buildings abound: Pakistan has one mosque for every

30 households; the United States has one house of worship for every 900 residents.[24] In addition, clinics, schools, orphanages, and other social institutions run by religious organizations give them a network of opportunities to shape development efforts. Confucian and Indian Vedic health care make important contributions to the health systems of China and India. And in the United States alone, member agencies of Catholic Charities spent more than $2.5 billion in 2000 to serve over nine million people—more than 3 percent of the population.[25]

Some exemplary cases of the use of religious wealth illustrate the impact religious institutions could have in helping to nudge the world toward sustainability. The Interfaith Center on Corporate Responsibility (ICCR), representing 275 Protestant, Catholic, and Jewish institutional investors in the United States, has been a leader for more than three decades in shaping corporate operating policies through the use of socially oriented shareholder resolutions.[26] (See Chapter 9.) More than half of such resolutions initiated in the United States in the past three years were filed or co-filed by religious groups; on more than a third of them, religious groups were the primary filers.[27] This role has caught the attention of secular activists on corporate responsibility. "One of the first things we do when we run a campaign is make sure that the ICCR is on board," says Tracey Rembert of the Shareholder Action Network, which advocates ethical investing and shareholder action.[28]

Asset #5: Social Capital

Finally, religion has a particular capacity to generate social capital—the bonds of trust, communication, cooperation, and information dissemination that create strong communities. Development economists began to recognize in the 1970s and 80s that economic development is fueled not just by stocks of land, labor, and financial capital, but also by education (human capital) and healthy ecosystems (ecological capital). By the 1990s, many theorists added social capital (community building) to the list because of its importance as a lubricant and glue in many communities: it greases the wheels of communication and interaction, which in turn strengthens the bonds that community members have with one another.[29]

While social capital is built by a broad range of groups in civil society, from political parties to civic clubs and hobby groups, religion is especially influential. Analyzing U.S. survey data, sociologist Andrew Greeley showed that religious institutions or persons, who are responsible for 34 percent of all volunteerism in the United States, fielded volunteers not just for religious work but for other society-building efforts as well.[30] About a third of the educational, political, youth, and human services volunteerism, a quarter of the health-related volunteerism, and a fifth of the employment-related volunteer work was undertaken by people motivated by their faith. The willingness to work for societal betterment, not just for the particular interests of a religious group, holds potential for the movement to build a sustainable world because environmental health is an issue of common concern for the planet and future generations that transcends religious and national differences.

The powerful religious toolbox for change has made religious groups a target for partnership by various secular organizations, including environmental ones. These partnerships tend to work best when religious groups are seen as full partners, and when groups appreciate the unique perspective—and unique value—that religious groups bring to the table. The environmentalist, for example, critiques consumerism largely because of its impact on forests, waterways, and air quality, while people of faith argue additionally that excessive attachment to the material world is harmful to a person's healthy development. The two arguments together pack a powerful punch in the effort to change consumer behavior and illustrate that religions add value, not just votes, to the sustainability movement.

© Klemens Kalischer

Indian Line Farm in Massachusetts, home of the first community-supported agriculture program in the United States.

PART TWO

Progress Re-Rooted

CHAPTER 4

New Vision:
Nature, Then Economies

*"If you take seriously those passages in the scripture
that say that we live by God's spirit and his breath, that we live,
move, and have our being in God, the implications for the
present economy are just devastating. Those passages call for
an entirely generous and careful economic life."*
—Wendell Berry[1]

T he Tlingit indigenous people of the U.S. state of Alaska use
the bark from cedar trees to make blankets, hats, baskets, floor
mats, and other goods, which makes cedar an important economic resource for them. But the harvesting is not your typical industrial process: before peeling away the bark, the Tlingit addresses the
spirits of the tree, a ritual that involves asking permission to take the
material. She describes what she is going to make, promises to take
only as much as she needs, and gives thanks for the resource. And
once the harvesting is complete, community members share their product extensively, a custom common to other Tlingit economic activities such as hunting and fishing.[2]

This attitude of humility, gratitude, and generosity distinguishes
the Tlingit economy's relationship to nature from that in industrial
economies. The Tlingit use the resource in a regenerative way: they
do not cut the entire cedar, but leave enough to ensure the tree's continued growth. (Trees are cut to make totems and canoes, but this is
relatively rare, carefully considered within the community, and, like
the harvesting of bark, enveloped in ritual.) Moreover, the promise

to utilize all the material that is gathered is a strikingly conservative approach to consumption. And their assumption that all of reality is infused with spirit—a worldview entirely foreign to modern economies—makes the Tlingit an awe-filled, spiritual economic actor.[3] "When we use the environment, it creates an obligation to our ancestors and to future generations," explains Dr. Rosita Worl, a Harvard-trained Tlingit anthropologist and president of the Sealaska Heritage Institute, which works to safeguard Tlingit culture.[4]

Imagine applying Tlinglit principles to modern-day economies. Suppose that every time a product designer, factory manager, or consumer uses an economic resource—when a car is designed, a batch of steel is ordered, or a paper towel is used—each of these economic actors gives a prayer of thanks for the resource bounty before them, and promises to use only as much as they really need. Their resource use would surely be more thoughtful and more conservative. And even if they see God manifested in nature differently than a Tlingit does, their understanding of resources and of economics would have a new spiritual dimension that would change the way each acts as an economic being.

Harvesting bark may not have a place in many industrial economies, but the principle of using resources within boundaries established by nature is broadly replicable today, and greatly needed. Economics in the 20th century produced enormously productive but also highly polluting and resource-intensive industrial economies. That model, commonly called neoclassical economics, remains dominant today, and indeed is being pursued by developing economies seeking their shot at prosperity. But key elements of the neoclassical approach cannot be sustained. And many elements of its worldview are arguably inconsistent with basic tenets of not only indigenous spiritual traditions, but formal religions as well.

Fortunately, alternative ways of building economies are being conceived that, like indigenous economies, work in harmony with nature, but at a level productive enough to meet the needs of a large global population. One approach, called ecological economics, borrows the best tools of neoclassical economics, such as markets, but uses them in an economy that is fundamentally bounded by nature and by the needs of people and their communities. Its starting assumptions, about the world and how people act in it, are different from those that underlie neoclassical economics. And from distinct starting points the two head in fundamentally different directions.

Nature, The Economic Base

If neoclassical economics were a theatrical performance, nature would be a bit actor: cheap, easily recruited, and largely overlooked. It appears briefly in the economy's opening act, supplying oil, wood, metals, fresh water, fertile soils, and other raw materials, and returns briefly at the end to absorb the economy's wastes. Despite its unglamorous role, nature is a dependable player, rarely missing a performance—and when it does, reliably supplying a substitute, according to the neoclassical perspective. Nature is also an undiscovered talent: its economic services such as flood protection, water filtering, erosion prevention, and the like never get a chance to shine on the neoclassical stage.

Societies have long had hints that nature deserves more attention and respect. Consider the problem of wastes. The London "fog" of 1952, in which severely polluted air killed thousands of people, and the fire on the Cuyahoga River in the U.S. state of Ohio in 1969, which was caused when oil and trash on its surface ignited, are extreme but illustrative examples of local environments being overused as waste dumps.[5] Today we know that the planet itself can be overloaded with waste: ozone depletion and climate change, for example, result from emitting more chemicals to our planet's atmosphere than it can absorb.

Meanwhile, nature's capacity to supply raw materials is clearly under stress with the peaking or near-peaking of oil supplies, and with demand for fish, water, and other key economic inputs surging to worrisome levels.[6] Whether substitutes can be found for these materials remains to be seen, but the challenge is huge: oil, for example, is the lifeblood of industrial economies, not just as a source of energy, but to supply innovative materials such as plastics. And water has no known substitute for its most vital applications, including slaking peoples' thirst, nurturing crops, and providing habitat and hydration for wildlife. In short, whether in supplying material or absorbing wastes, the natural environment poses real constraints to human ambitions to build ever-larger economies.

Ecological economists are vocal advocates of the commonsensical idea that nature's capacity to supply raw materials or clean up waste is limited. But they also work hard to reveal nature's hidden talents, the multitude of services that support human economies. Consider just three examples. Wetlands act as catchments for excess rainfall, preventing floods or reducing their severity. Indeed, ecologists assert that the fundamental infrastructure failure of the 2005 Hurricane Katrina disaster was not crumbling levees, but the loss of buffering wetlands decades earlier that were sacrificed to urban expansion.[7] Or think of the bees, butterflies, bats, and hummingbirds that pollinate flowers, with direct benefits to us all: researchers at the Forgotten Pollinators Campaign estimate that one of every three bites of food we consume is provided through pollination services.[8] And of course trees absorb carbon dioxide, purifying the air we breathe and preventing the planet from overheating. In the mid-1990s, ecological economist Robert Costanza estimated the cost of replicating nature's services using human-built infrastructure and technologies. His conservative calculation: $33 trillion, nearly twice the value of output of the global economy at the time.[9] (Many of nature's services, of course, cannot be replicated at any price.)

The take-home lesson is that all economic activity is rooted in the natural environment, and is deeply dependent on it. This assertion may seem like common sense—can you think of an economic activity that is *not* grounded in nature, that does *not* use raw materials or emit wastes?—but it turns neoclassical thinking about nature on its head. Far from being a bit extra, nature has a starring role in economic dramas everywhere. It deserves attention commensurate with the importance of its role. Indeed, factoring nature into our production and consumption is indispensable if the prosperity of the 20th century is to continue into the future.

Ecological economics folds the health of natural systems into its planning from the very beginning. For example, a company thinking of building a new highway, housing subdivision, or electronic product line, or an individual contemplating buying a new car or moving to a new house, would consider a new set of issues. A business person's concerns center not just on the expected rate of return on an investment or the market potential of a new product. And a consumer would look beyond sticker price and mortgage rates. From an ecological economics perspective, the impact of business and lifestyle decisions on the natural environment takes on elementary importance, so that levels of recycled content, energy efficiency, and waste generation become vital questions.

The Question of Size

Because ecological economics views economies as embedded in nature, rather than the other way around, nature is the boundary setter: economic growth will ultimately be limited by the availability of forest area or water, farmland or oil, and by the capacity of the atmosphere, rivers, oceans, and landfills to absorb our wastes. Studies over the past decade or more have begun to outline what those boundaries are. Ecologist Peter Vitousek and colleagues at Stanford, for example, estimated in 1986 that human activities were already appropriating some 25 percent of the planet's net primary productivity (NPP)—the net growth of all plants in a year—and 40 percent of the land-based NPP.[10] A similar study in 1997 led by water specialist Sandra Postel found that humans were appropriating a little more than half of the world's accessible freshwater supplies.[11]

Because nature itself needs to use natural resources—plants and fish need water, too—and because our planet and its resources are finite, the question of how big human economies can get looms large. The question becomes even more pressing in light of the projected 40 percent increase in global population in coming decades, the aspirations of developing countries for higher standards of living, and the seeming endless consumption in wealthy countries, all of which step up resource demands.[12] Given the predicament, it seems clear that economic growth, at least of the resource-intensive kind, cannot continue indefinitely.

This may seem a chilling conclusion, an assault on our very assumptions about what is good in an economy. After all, we are comforted when the stock market is up and when gross national product is booming, and we worry about unemployment and recession when barometers head the other direction. But the "no-more-growth" conclusion need not lead to despair, especially if we speak about growth more precisely. It is growth in the use of virgin materials and fossil fuels, the pieces of economic activity that degrade the environment, which cannot continue. If we imagine building economies largely around the materials already in our economy, through recycling and other clever strategies, and if we do so in clean ways, say through renewable energy, a clean growth is still possible, and will be indispensable in the poorest countries whose economies need growth to deliver the opportunity for a dignified life for all.

This vision of a "materials-lite" economic future is challenging, but it is not a pipe dream. Researchers in the 1990s estimated that resource use in industrial countries could be reduced four- to tenfold in any number of creative ways, many of which are beginning to be practiced.[13] These diverse initiatives all have one thing in common: they deliver the services people are getting today, but with greatly reduced use of materials and energy. Consider some of the imaginative ideas companies are pursuing:

- *Design for recycling*—Designers create products whose components have bar-code labels describing their material makeup, which makes it easier and more economical to recycle them later. The European Union, for example, has mandated that 95 percent of materials in automobiles will be reusable or recoverable by 2015.[14] *Bottom line:* consumers get the car they are after, but with less need for virgin steel and other materials.

- *Design for remanufacture*—Designers make products easy to dismantle for repair and refurbishing, extending the life of still-functioning components in a refurbished unit. Xerox does this with its copiers.[15] *Bottom line:* consumers get the copying service they are after, but with less impact on the environment.

- *Lease rather than sell*—Companies supply customers with the service they are after, rather than a product, if possible. The Interface carpet company's carpet leasing program provides carpet to customers and replaces individual carpet tiles as needed.

Used tiles are then taken and recycled back by Interface.[16] *Bottom line:* people get the service they seek, with little stress on the environment.

- *Promote institutionalized sharing*—In Europe and the United States, car-sharing companies provide clean, fueled, and well-maintained cars in neighborhoods and near transit centers for occasional use.[17] *Bottom line:* people get the occasional, private transportation they need without a second car—or in some cases, a first car.
- *Industrial parks*—Companies locate near other companies that can take their wastes and reuse them, greatly reducing waste flows. In Kalundborg, Denmark, warm water from a power plant is used in a nearby fish farm, sludge from the fish farm fertilizes farmland, and fly ash from the power plant is used to make cement.[18] *Bottom line:* companies produce the same quantity of goods, with reduced levels of waste.

In all cases, the companies continue to grow. But their growth increasingly consists of providing the services people need, rather than an endless stream of goods.

Should Religions Care?

Teachings on the role of nature in an economy are not particularly specific in many traditions, with indigenous traditions a standout exception. But it is clear that religions regard nature as more than a mere warehouse for the world's economies. In Muslim teachings, for example, the principle of trusteeship is important: the world is created for human use, but people have a responsibility to use it with great care. This is similar to the teaching of stewardship in the Jewish and Christian tradition. (The meaning of stewardship is debated in Jewish and Christian circles, but most agree that it involves obligations of care by humans for the natural environment.)

Similarly, while the neoclassical perspective maintains that private property, without restrictions, is ethical and necessary for development, religious thinking often attaches obligations to those rights. In Muslim thought, for example, private property is subject to the interest of the community. Goods of particular public interest, such as "water and pasturage and fire," should be state enterprises. And from a Christian, particularly Catholic, perspective, private property is permitted but is to be used with adequate regard for the public good.

In the neoclassical worldview, material goods exist to provide pleasure, but religious views of the role of goods are different. In the Buddhist worldview, consumption is merely a means to well-being: the goal is actually to use as *few* goods as possible to maximize well-being.[19] For a Muslim, material goods are meant to be useful to humans, but within clear boundaries. The devotee is required to give regularly to charity, to avoid extravagant spending, and to avoid spending on alcohol, pork, or gambling, and on capital goods that carry interest charges.[20]

Finally, it is worth noting that neoclassical and ecological economics also diverge on non-ecological issues of vital importance to religion. Where the individual is the basic actor in neoclassical economics, individuals in ecological economics and in many religions are seen as relational beings who are rooted in community. Buddhist teaching, for example, describes the individual as a free actor, but one who must have a spirit of compassion: the Buddhist ethic of Bodhisattva urges that people act in a way that benefits all beings.[21] In Christian and Muslim thought, similarly, the mandate to love one's neighbor is fundamental.

A Wholesale Economic Makeover

By placing the environment at the center of our economies, ecological economists revolutionize our understanding of progress. In their worldview, economic tools from the neoclassical perspective, such as the market, still play an important role, but their use is bounded by rules and goals set by society at large. In the process, a new society is created, one that preserves the gains of the last century but builds on them and makes them sustainable.

Theologian Sallie McFague, in her 2001 book *Life Abundant: Rethinking Theology and Economy for a Planet in Peril*, gives a sense of what this new society would look like: "Everything must change— from where we grow our lettuce (nearby, not thousands of miles away) to how we drive our cars (by fuel cell, not combustible engine), from how we educate our children (to be ecologically literate) to who gets medical care (everyone), from how we use the land (sharing it with other species) to how we envision God (as the source of the good life for all)." McFague draws a clear distinction between this vision and the reality of economies and societies today. "Just as we are defined now as consumers and see our planet in terms of consumption, so if we lived within the alternative model, we would define ourselves as household members and would see our planet as the home within which we all must live now and in the future. Who we think we are matters, both for our own good life and for planetary wellbeing."[22]

CHAPTER 5

Nature as Sacred Ground

"Everybody needs beauty as well as bread,
places to play in and pray in, where nature
may heal and give strength to body and soul."
—John Muir[1]

t is true that the world's religious (but not indigenous) traditions have largely come to environmental issues late in the game. Roughly a century after John Muir and Theodore Roosevelt spearheaded the conservation movement in the United States, 40 years after Aldo Leopold published his land ethic *A Sand County Almanac*, and 30 years after Rachel Carson's classic *Silent Spring* appeared, religious denominations were just beginning to emerge as concerned players regarding environmental issues.

But when religious groups get involved, they do so in powerful ways. Consider Sacred Gifts for a Living Planet, a program established by the Alliance of Religions and Conservation (ARC) and WWF International as a way for religious traditions to make environmental offerings—from pledges to conserve landholdings to adoption of renewable energy—as a way to help celebrate the turn of the new century. The idea was attractive: it built on WWF's successful "Gifts to the Earth" program, a high-profile effort to recognize government projects and other actions that favored the environment. "Sacred Gifts" tapped the power of gift as a religious concept—"all of our assets are gifts from God," observes Martin Palmer, Secretary General of ARC.[2] Furthermore, by linking Sacred Gifts to the celebration of the new millennium, ARC and WWF fueled the program with a high level of energy, publicity, and participation.

Some 42 Sacred Gifts had been made as of early 2005, each as different in character as the religions and denominations that offered them.[3] They include:

- A ban on hunting snow leopards by Mongolian Buddhists, and the creation of sacred forests where logging is banned.
- A declaration by Catholic bishops in the U.S. Pacific Northwest of the need to protect the Columbia River watershed.
- Environmental audits of synagogues in the U.K., coordinated by the Board of Deputies, the highest Jewish authority in the country.
- A commitment by Zoroastrians in India to recycle flower offerings from Fire Temples in vermiculture projects, the product of which is used in the garden areas of the temple.
- Establishment of a Center for Islam and Ecology at a university in Wales.
- A pledge by the Maronite Church in Lebanon to preserve the Harissa Forest, which it owns, from further exploitation and degradation.
- A pledge by the United Methodist Church in the United States to eliminate use of chlorine-bleached paper, and to lobby a nationwide printing and photocopying company to offer chlorine-free paper to customers.
- A pledge by the Jains to rebuild a village that was destroyed in a 2001 earthquake in Gujarat, India.

Of the original 26 gifts made in 2000, 20 have either achieved their goals or are well on their way. Another round of 16 gifts was added in 2003, and the success rate is higher than for the original group. A third round of gifts is being organized for 2007, and Palmer anticipates that the Chinese government will be involved, centering on a sacred mountain in Qinling. The government, Palmer reports, sees religion as an important societal player, and views environmental issues as an acceptable arena for religious involvement.[4]

Indeed, in the past 20 years, religions have begun to play key, even leadership, roles on the environmental stage, through grassroots projects, theological treatises, collaborations with secular environmental programs, and inclusion of environmental themes in worship and on liturgical calendars. It is possible to overstate the level of engagement—outside of indigenous traditions, the environment is still not a major concern across any entire religion or denomination. But interest is growing quickly in pockets of activity within all of the world's major religions, as religions begin to ratify or reassess their understanding of humans in the environment, and as they begin to give the environment a prominent place in their worldviews.

Views on the Place of Nature

The world's religions view the environment in different ways (see Sidebar 5–1, p. 70), but all are paying increasing attention to the natural world, as evidence of widespread degradation continues to pour forth.[5] The planetary scale of the crisis has awakened a process that Mary Evelyn Tucker of the Forum on Religion and Ecology describes as the retrieval, re-evaluation, and reconstruction of religious wisdom regarding human interaction with the natural world. In other words, religious traditions are finding in their own codex of wisdom ancient teachings that may have been overlooked, or that are understood more profoundly in the light of the global environmental crisis. Her analysis suggests that religions are more adaptable, even as they work to reveal eternal truths, than they are commonly perceived to be.[6]

For example, the longstanding concern of the World Council of Churches (WCC) for the "vulnerable and suffering" now extends to a suffering environment in addition to suffering people, according to David Hallman of the WCC's climate change program. He explains that theological reflection that begins with a community's "lived experience" (the approach that WCC uses in its work) must, in the modern context, include the reality of a seriously damaged planet. This change in orientation gives environmental issues—polar bears threatened by loss of habitat as the Arctic warms, or coral reefs under threat of die-off, for example—a high profile at the Council, in part because of their impact on human well-being, but also because the environment itself is now seen as a "vulnerable and suffering" part of God's creation.[7]

Religious interest in environmental issues, whether longstand-

SIDEBAR 5–1. Selected Religious Perspectives on Nature

In the three western monotheistic traditions—Judaism, Christianity, and Islam—morality has traditionally been human-focused, with nature being of secondary importance and with God transcending the natural world. Thus, the natural world can be seen as a set of resources for human use, a perspective that some observers blame for the wasteful and destructive development of the past two centuries.

Yet scholars in each of these traditions find substantial grounds for building a strong environmental ethic. The Judaic concept of a covenant or legal agreement between God and humanity, for example, can be extended to all of creation. The Christian foci on sacrament and incarnation are seen as lenses through which the entire natural world can be viewed as sacred. And the Islamic concept of vice-regency teaches that the natural world is not owned by humans but is given to them in trust—a trust that implies certain responsibilities to preserve the balance of creation.

Hinduism and Buddhism in South Asia contain teachings concerning the natural world that are arguably in conflict. Some scholars in these traditions emphasize the illusory nature of the material world and the desirability of escaping suffering by turning to a timeless world of spirit (in the case of Hinduism) or by seeking release in nirvana (in the case of some meditative schools of Buddhism). This other-worldly orientation, some scholars argue, minimizes the importance of environmental degradation.

On the other hand, both religions place great emphasis on correct conduct and on fulfillment of duty, which often includes obligations to environmental preservation. Thus, Hindus regard rivers as sacred and, in the concept of *lila*, the creative play of the gods, Hindu theology engages the world as a creative manifestation of the divine. Meanwhile, Buddhist environmentalists often stress the importance of trees in the life of the Buddha, and "socially engaged" Buddhism in Asia and the United States is

active in environmental protection, especially of forests. Moreover, the Mahayana schools of Buddhism emphasize the interde-
pendent nature of reality in such images as the jeweled net of
Indra, in which each jewel reflects all the others in the universe.

The East Asian traditions of Confucianism and Daoism
seamlessly link the divine, human, and natural worlds. The
divine is not seen as transcendent; instead, the Earth's fecundity
is seen as continuously unfolding through nature's movements
across the seasons and through human workings in the cycles of
agriculture. This organic worldview is centered around the concept of *ch'i*, the dynamic, material force that infuses the natural
and human worlds, unifying matter and spirit. Confucianists and
Daoists seek to live in harmony with nature and with other
human beings, while paying attention to the movements of the
Dao, the Way. Despite the affinity of these traditions with an environmental ethic, however, deforestation, pollution, and other
forms of degradation have become widespread in contemporary
East Asia due to many factors, including rapid industrialization
and the decline of traditional values in the last 50 years with the
spread of Communism.

Finally, indigenous traditions, closely tied to their local bioregion for food and for materials for clothing, shelter, and cultural
activities, tend to have their environmental ethics embedded in
their worldviews. Gratitude for the fecundity of nature is a common feature of their cultures. Ritual calendars are often derived
from the cycles of nature, such as the appearance of the sun or
moon, or the seasonal return of certain animals or plants.
Indigenous traditions often have a very light environmental footprint compared with industrial societies. Still, many indigenous
traditions recall times of environmental degradation in their
mythologies. Since the colonial period, the efforts of indigenous
people to live sustainably in their homelands have been hurt by
the encroachment of settlements and by logging, mining, and
other forms of resource exploitation.

Source: See Endnote 5 for Chapter 5.

ing or more recent, is typically reflected in a diverse range of initiatives that can be classified into three major areas emphasizing education, infrastructure, and advocacy.

Education and Behavior Change

Environmental Catechism

Education of congregations is probably the most active area of "green" religious activity. At the most basic level, religious leaders are engaged in disseminating environmental teaching through statements and declarations to the faithful and to the public at large. In the United States, statements with an environmental focus are no longer unusual from religious groups. Since 1950, member churches of the National Council of Churches (NCC) have issued some 133 declarations on everything from toxics to climate change, with 100 of these, or 75 percent, having been issued since 1985.[8]

Some religious schools are incorporating environmental education into their curriculum (see Sidebar 5–2), but most religious educational activity happens directly in the church, synagogue, or mosque.[9] In the United States, member organizations of the National Religious Partnership on the Environment, which is made up of the NCC, the Coalition on the Environment and Jewish Life (COEJL), the Evangelical Environmental Network, and the U.S. Conference of Catholic Bishops, have developed denomination-specific educational resources and made them available to local houses of worship nationwide. Some resources are extensive: of the nearly 150 environmental programs from Jewish groups around the United States that are listed on the COEJL website, more than 90 percent are educational.[10] Meanwhile, the Islamic Foundation for Ecology and Environmental Sciences provides resources for use at mosques and Islamic education centers on environmental issues, including a newsletter called Eco-Islam.[11]

Education also happens through worship services, and some religions and denominations are developing worship-oriented resources with an environmental focus. The NCC makes worship aids available for Earth Sunday (the Sunday closest to Earth Day, April 22) and the Unitarian Universalist church puts out a 200-page worship

SIDEBAR 5–2. **Earth, Faith, and Justice at a School in Brazil**

At Colegio Santa Maria, a private school in São Paulo, Brazil, run by the Sisters of the Holy Cross, the environment is not a course or an extracurricular club, but is woven throughout the curriculum, whether a student is two-years old or an adult attending night classes. "Environmentalism...penetrates all of the disciplines, and is part of the air we breathe," Sister Diane Cundiff, the principal, explains.

The school also finds environmentalism to be closely linked to the faith and justice values on which the school is based. "Nobody here at the school would separate taking care of the environment from taking care of people," says Sister Diane. "The planet belongs to humanity. Justice and non-violence won't happen until the planet belongs to everyone." She makes the faith connection quickly: "If we don't preserve Creation, we are not preserving life, and that goes against our Christian responsibility."

Sister Diane and the school's staff are motivated by the Earth Charter, a global effort to develop a set of ethical guidelines for progress in the 21st century. "You can't read it without seeing God...You could read the whole thing and say 'this is the Word of God,' and everyone would say 'Amen.'" Since 2001, faculty have used one of the four pillars of the Earth Charter— respect and care for the community of life; ecological integrity; social and economic justice; and democracy, non-violence, and peace—each semester as an organizing frame for class content. This was not easy: the faculty found that it was "impossible to do one pillar without bringing in the other pillars. They are all connected," says Sister Diane.

Sister Diane offers examples of how environment and justice are made a part of daily instruction:

- A viaduct that flows through the school often carries sewage water originating in a slum some 20 kilometers away. The students test the water at the school as part of their science work. They also go to the slums to teach residents to test the water, as a way to help people avoid getting sick.
- Students are taught to avoid waste and to separate their garbage into color-coded depositories for paper, metal,

glass, and non-recyclables. But they are also taught to cast a critical eye on the material: Is everything that gets thrown away really waste? To answer this, they work with the local waste pickers' cooperative to identify art projects, toys, plants, and clothing that can be reused. Trash isn't always trash, the students learn.

- Students spend a few weeks of their summer vacation working in poor areas to teach recycling concepts, including how to build a compost heap, and to tend a garden, with the goal of reducing food costs in those areas and increasing nutrition levels.
- Fifth graders researching alternative energy technologies adapted a simple water heating technology to provide hot water at the school. Originally developed at a local university for demonstration at the Earth Summit in Rio in 1992, the heater consists of a water box and a system of pipes through which the water circulates, without requiring electricity. An unemployed engineer helped the kids adapt the technology. The students, in turn, have shown residents of nearby slums how to build the devices, saving them energy and money.

The school's impact is felt outside of São Paulo as well. In northeast Brazil, where clean water is often scarce, many children die from diseases linked to contaminated water. Cisterns can help residents collect rainwater and keep it clean, but the materials to build them are too expensive for many residents. Students at Colegio Santa Maria make sandwiches at the school and sell them in São Paulo, then send the proceeds to the northeast for use in cistern construction.

Sister Diane's experience at the school has even influenced her own, worldwide religious order. She and other Sisters of the Holy Cross decided at their worldwide congregation meeting in July 2004 to adopt the Earth Charter as a guiding document for their various ministries. Some of the sisters were not convinced, feeling that a document with an environmental focus would limit their work in myriad non-environmental ministries. "If you say this, you haven't read it," Sister Diane told her fellow sisters.

Source: See Endnote 9 for Chapter 5.

resource called "Honoring Earth." In some cases, worship activities have a direct political connection: the Alliance of Religions and Conservation has developed a liturgy focused on passage of European Union legislation designed to register, evaluate, and authorize or eliminate chemicals in Europe. Part of the liturgy is the "Rainbow Covenant," a prayer in which worshipers pledge to work against the destruction of other living beings. Finally, the Greek Orthodox Church has incorporated environmental focus into its liturgical calendar. Since 1989, it has celebrated September 1st as Creation Day.

Driving the Point Home

Not all religious environmental education takes place in a house of worship. In 2002, the Evangelical Environmental Network (EEN), an organization of environmentally oriented evangelical Christians in the United States, hit upon a novel way to draw attention to the moral dimension of automobile ownership. Its "What Would Jesus Drive?" campaign echoed a familiar question—What would Jesus do?—that is used as a moral barometer by many Christians, and in doing so tapped some of the question's moral power. The EEN campaign asked people to be aware of the environmental toll of automobile use, and to take this moral dimension into account in their next car purchase.

To publicize the campaign, EEN director Reverend Jim Ball drove a hybrid car from Texas to Washington, D.C., in 2003, stopping to meet with political leaders and the media along the way. In Dallas, for example, he met with two city council members and urged them to work to make the city government's car fleet all-hybrid. He made the same pitch to the mayor of Little Rock, Arkansas, and to an aide to that state's governor. In his online journal, Ball notes that he learned during the trip that "our message is sound. Once people hear our position they find it hard to argue with." [12] The extensive media exposure made Ball's trip a rolling classroom for environmental education from a religious perspective.

A Captive Audience

A similarly creative environmental education initiative is the shipboard symposia series run by the Ecumenical Patriarch Bartholomew, symbolic leader of the 250-million-member Christian Orthodox Church. Dubbed "the Green Patriarch" because of his high-profile advocacy on environmental issues, Bartholomew has focused heavily on water-related environmental issues through sailing seminars every few years since 1996. To date, the voyages have studied the problems of the Danube River and of the Aegean, Black, Adriatic, and Baltic Seas, with a trip on the Amazon River in the summer of 2006.

Aboard a chartered ship for approximately one week, scientists, theologians, policymakers, and journalists hear dozens of lectures on the aquatic region under study. The participants tend to be influential: in addition to the Patriarch, the 2002 Adriatic Sea symposium included a special consultant to the United Nations Secretary-General, the former head of the U.N. Environment Programme, the head of the U.N. Development Programme, two Roman Catholic cardinals, the Primate of the Church of Sweden, imams from Egypt and Syria, a sheikh from Albania and the grand imam of Bosnia Herzegovina, several ambassadors, several heads of environmental and development-oriented NGOs, the president of the U.N. Foundation, and some 40 journalists. Sharing meals and living quarters, lectures, and field trips, these high-profile participants and other attendees learn and network with each other, to impressive effect. The Adriatic symposium ended in Venice with the Ecumenical Patriarch and Pope John Paul II signing a joint declaration on environmental protection.[13]

The gatherings focus on bodies of water in real trouble, such as the Black Sea, now the most degraded marine area in Europe. Damage to the sea, described as "catastrophic," has resulted from several decades' worth of coastal development, invasion of exotic species, damming of rivers feeding the sea, and the growing burden of fertilizer runoff and other pollutants.[14] The 1997 symposium visited ports in six countries, sponsored field trips to degraded areas, and offered some two-dozen lectures.[15] Beyond building relationships among scientists and religious leaders and raising public environmental awareness through the hundreds of news reports generated by participating journalists, the trip inspired concrete initiatives on behalf of the environment. It gave rise to the Halki Ecological Institute, for example, a two-week-long program in 1999 to introduce Orthodox priests, seminary students, and journalists to the environmental ills of the Black Sea. The World Bank increased funding for a Black Sea program, one of its few grant (as distinguished from loan) initiatives, largely because a World Bank vice president was at the 1997 symposium.[16]

Similar fruit was borne of the 1999 symposium on the Danube River. Participants testify to the role of this gathering in creating a sense of connection among the people of the river's nine host countries, even in the face of the ongoing Yugoslav war. "Divided peoples felt united by the river," explains Philip Weller, then a WWF program director of the Danube Carpathian project and a symposium participant. "The symposium helped people to feel connected to nature." This emotional connection was possible because of the great interest generated by the Ecumenical Patriarch's participation. "People are still talking about...the Patriarch's involvement, three years after the event," notes another participant. The Patriarch's leadership is a prime example of how the moral authority of religion might be focused on building a sustainable world.[17]

Greening of Infrastructure and Assets

Because religious institutions tend to use large buildings and often own extensive tracts of land, greening their operations can help lighten society's environmental impact, while serving as models for other institutions or individuals interested in lightening their own impact. Religions are increasingly aware of their potential for environmental good, and some are taking creative actions to green their operations.

One powerful example of environmentally sensitive land use is the Living Churchyards and Cemetery project in the United Kingdom. More than 6,000 British churchyards—the plots of land that sit adjacent to churches and are often used as burial grounds—are now managed as "sacred ecosystems," without pesticides and with infrequent mowing, in order to provide habitat for birds, reptiles, and insects where little habitat may have existed for perhaps hundreds of years.[18] The yards are respected as historical, cultural, and ecological sites that provide for the needs of mourners and wildlife alike. They also become a natural classroom for helping parishioners understand the wildlife in their area, an especially valuable service in urban churchyards.[19]

In India, meanwhile, Sikhs have taken the first steps in an initiative to reduce fossil fuels used in their 28,000 *gurdwaras*, or temples. The move is part of the Cycle of the Environment, a 300-year period begun in 1999 that guides Sikh activities. (It replaces the Cycle of the Sword, which ran from 1699 to 1999.) As is the Sikh custom, each gurdwara runs a free kitchen called a *langar* where anyone can come for a meal. The langars feed an estimated 30 million people daily—and in the process, consume a lot of fuel. The Sikh community has committed to outfitting langars with solar-powered electricity and making their cooking equipment more energy efficient. The hope is that they will see savings of 15 percent in fuel use for their hospitality services.[20]

Clean Energy

Probably one of the most successful faith-driven sustainability initiatives in the United States is Interfaith Power and Light (IPL), the flagship program of the San Francisco-based Regeneration Project. IPL coordinates congregation-based programs that encourage energy conservation, the use of renewable energy, and advocacy for green energy and to combat climate change. Founded in 1997 as Episcopal Power and Light by the Reverend Sally Bingham, and re-launched in 2001 as Interfaith Power and Light, IPL now has 19 state chapters, plus one in the District of Columbia, with more than 30 denominations and religions represented.[21]

For several reasons, IPL is an outstanding example of the potential of religious groups to promote change. It frames energy and climate as legitimate issues of faith, taps into the network of religious congregations across the country to multiply its influence, and draws on a broad set of tools and activities to advance its mission.[22] (See Table 5–1.) IPL's success after just a decade or so of operation suggests that widespread embrace of the IPL model by the religious community could move renewable energy and climate change policy ahead in the United States at a lightning pace.

Reverend Bingham, who was ordained only in her fifties, got involved in faith-based environmentalism because, "I came to the conclusion that the religious community...had not stepped up to the plate

TABLE 5–1. **Activities of Interfaith Power and Light**

Green Buildings

IPL congregations frequently take steps to green their facilities. Michigan IPL reported in 2006 that its congregations' efficiency improvements and renewable energy choices had saved more than $775,000 and eliminated the same amount of pollution as planting 612 hectares of forest or removing 960 cars from the road. Some 25 churches and synagogues in Connecticut IPL have purchased clean energy, and 9 of these have run campaigns to encourage congregants to choose clean energy for their homes.

Technical Assistance

Greater Washington IPL is working to survey 190 Washington, D.C. congregations to determine their interest in doing an energy audit of their facilities. Connecticut IPL has arranged for technical assistance on green building or energy conservation projects for 22 organizations, including 20 congregations, a kosher food store, and the state association of non-profit building managers.

Media

State IPL leaders regularly do interviews with radio and print media and write op-ed pieces about energy and climate issues. IPLs sometimes coordinate on op-eds—leaders seized upon Russia's ratification of Kyoto in 2005 to get op-eds placed in California and New York, for example. Fourteen state IPLs have websites; many others have professional displays and outreach videos, including one called "Lighten Up," that are used to recruit members.

Trainings and Conferences

National IPL conferences gather state leaders to share ideas, build relationships, and get training in media relations, fundraising, and lobbying. The 2005 gathering generated a Great Lakes regional effort to link IPLs in the upper Midwest.

Advocacy Work

Several IPLs have lobbied state and federal officials on renewable energy and climate change. Illinois IPL has run a campaign

TABLE 5–1 CONTINUED

to mobilize support for the state's (voluntary) 8 percent renewable portfolio standard, while Oregon IPL used letter writing, a clergy-endorsed petition, and meetings with the governors of Oregon and California to press for strong state action on climate change. Attendees at the 2005 IPL national conference in Washington met with 42 members of Congress to discuss the moral reasons for a clean energy program and push for real solutions to global warming.

Sale of Merchandise
Michigan IPL has a website with an online shopping cart that allows congregations to choose high-efficiency appliances and lighting. Promoting compact fluorescent light bulbs is popular, as when 30 Connecticut congregations banded together in a "Lighten-Up" sales campaign in 2005, selling thousands of bulbs.

Recruitment
IPL congregation leaders spread the energy efficiency message to other churches, synagogues, and other houses of worship, often giving dozens of talks each year outside of their own community. IPLs as a whole are well on their way to doubling their congregational membership in 2006.

Source: See Endnote 22 for Chapter 5.

on one of the great moral issues of our time." For Bingham, religious involvement in environmentalism is as important as it is late. "If the religious community is not involved" in the sustainability movement, she observes, "the transformation will not happen. Without that voice, we are not going to make change happen."[23]

Potential for Savings

Conservation programs like the ones used in IPLs could have real environmental impact. Andy Rudin of the Interfaith Coalition on Energy (ICE), which has been in business since 1982 advising some 4,200 congregations in the Philadelphia area on ways to reduce energy use, notes that participants in the program have reduced their energy usage by an average of 10 percent. This includes the congregations that signed up, but did not take action after becoming involved with ICE, which suggests that a 10 percent reduction is a very conservative estimate of the potential energy savings at churches across the United States. "We've seen congregations achieve 50 percent savings," says Rudin.[24]

"Off" is the key, Rudin explains. "Turning off the lights inside a soda machine may save $300 per year. Who needs to chill drinking water in the winter? Why do steeple lights have to be lit when no one is awake to see them? Why not allow worship spaces to have the same temperature swings as naturally occur in the spring, summer, and fall?"[25]

Indeed, the savings across the country could be substantial, given the more than 307,000 houses of worship that exist in the United States.[26] The U.S. Environmental Protection Agency estimates that congregations serious about energy savings could achieve reductions of 25–30 percent.[27] This would have real meaning for the environment, and for the bottom line of churches. EPA estimates savings of half a billion dollars to the congregations, an average of more than $1,600 per church, synagogue, or mosque. More importantly, a 25 percent reduction in energy use at churches would have the same impact on pollution as removing a million cars from the roads or planting nearly 570,000 hectares of trees. And it would make more than 13.5 billion kilowatt-hours of electricity available for other uses, without the construction of new power plants.[28] Add to this the savings achieved by congregants inspired to pursue energy efficiency or green energy at home, and the savings nationwide could be substantial.

Political Activism

Religious groups have become active in direct political activity on behalf of the environment as well. Sometimes advocacy is motivated by a deep concern for the integrity of the natural environment. Other times it is a response to the religious imperative to advocate for justice.

In 1995, the Evangelical Environmental Network in the United States used the political power of evangelicals to save the Endangered Species Act (ESA) from being significantly weakened. Their media strategy was brilliant. Calvin DeWitt, an evangelical professor of environmental studies at the University of Wisconsin, Madison, framed the issue as "the Noah's ark of our day," and charged that "Congress and special interests are trying to sink it."[29] The ESA was saved, and many give credit to EEN for persuading conservative Republicans that an important religious constituency was supportive of saving species, or, in terms more meaningful for evangelicals, "God's Creation." EEN, together with an interfaith group called the Noah Alliance, are once again involved in protecting the ESA from renewed attempts to weaken it.[30]

Meanwhile, the interfaith group GreenFaith makes advocacy, guided by a carefully developed statement of advocacy policy, one of its principal program thrusts. Executive Director Reverend Fletcher Harper, for example, has testified at a hearing of the New Jersey Department of Environmental Protection in favor of classifying carbon dioxide, a greenhouse gas, as a pollutant.[31] GreenFaith has also joined two environmental organizations in a lawsuit against the U.S. Army Corps of Engineers over dredging in Newark Bay, which would likely release dioxin and other toxins.[32] And it is working with other environmental groups to reduce diesel emissions in the state by 75 percent.[33] Harper and the GreenFaith board see the advocacy work as part of their religious call to justice, and as a natural complement to their efforts to encourage green building and environmental education.

Hungry for Justice

A more recent, high-profile example of religious pressure to influence environmental policy comes from Brazil, where Bishop Luis Flavio Cappio, head of the diocese of Barra in the state of Bahia, started a hunger strike in September 2005 to protest government plans for the San Francisco River. The bishop demanded that the government live up to its commitment to "revitalize" the river, which had suffered increased siltation because of extensive deforestation along its banks. The president of Brazil, Luiz Inácio Lula da Silva, was also in favor of the river's revitalization, but said this would happen only after a major project to transfer water from the San Francisco to drier states in Brazil's northeast was completed. The bishop, who was not necessarily opposed to the water transfer plan, wanted restoration of the river to occur first.

The bishop's stance is part of a growing trend toward religious involvement in environmental issues in Brazil. In recent years, some theologians, ministers, priests, and nuns have embraced ecological concerns, in some cases putting their lives at risk. Sister Dorothy Stang, for example, worked for decades in the Amazon region defending peasants' land rights and their ecological use of forests—and in the process, making enemies of loggers. They put an $18,000 bounty on her life, and in 2005 she was shot to death by agents of illegal logging interests.[34]

In this context, Bishop Cappio may have felt emboldened to take religious environmental commitment to a new level. Having a bishop involved automatically gave the issue a high profile, and having the support of the National Conference of Bishops multiplied the power of his stance. Moreover, his use of a hunger strike was unusual for clergy, especially for a bishop. And he directly took on the president—a left-leaning politician with strong environmental credentials—over what was essentially an issue of timing (restoration first vs. water transfers first).

In the end, a compromise was reached and Bishop Cappio ended his hunger strike. But the fact that the bishop was willing to "give my life for the San Francisco River and its people," in his words, and use the full force of his position as a bishop, suggests his passion for the river—and an unusually high level of religious commitment to the environment.

CHAPTER 6

Warming to the Climate Challenge

"Humanity is conducting an unintended, uncontrolled,
globally pervasive experiment whose ultimate consequences
could be second only to a global nuclear war."
—WMO, UNEP, and Environment Canada[1]

For more than two decades, a debate has raged in parliaments, boardrooms, classrooms, and pubs around the world: is climate change for real? For a group of South Pacific Islanders, the debate ended in August 2004. That was when the community of Lateu in the island nation of Vanuatu moved their village—houses, furniture, personal possessions, village water pumps, and other infrastructure, even the church—more than 500 meters inland because of rising seas created by a warming global climate.[2] The United Nations Environment Programme describes the move as one of the first cases of a formal displacement of an entire population because of climate change.[3]

Lateu villagers have been dealing with the effects of a warming climate for about two decades, and rising sea level only begins to describe their problems. Tropical cyclones have produced "king tides" high enough to damage residents' homes.[4] Salt water has penetrated the village's underground supply of fresh water. People became increasingly vulnerable to water-borne diseases and skin infections.[5] And the coast has eroded some 2–3 meters per year, with more than 50 meters of coastline in total surrendered to rising seas.[6] The worsening situation gradually persuaded villagers that major changes were afoot that could no longer be ignored.

The local church was a key player in making the connection between the growing list of village problems, on one hand, and climate change, on the other. The South Pacific Regional Environment Program, recognizing the important role the church played in Vanuatu, had been working for years with church groups and other nongovernmental institutions to educate villagers throughout the South Pacific about the changes to their islands—and later, to prepare them for the move.[7] By one press account, it was when church leaders made plans to relocate the village church inland that villagers became convinced of the gravity of the situation.[8]

Lateu is a small village—just 100 people—on a small island in an isolated South Pacific nation. But its story is a parable of the extraordinary issues raised by a warming climate: stark changes to ecosystems, difficult adaptations by humans and other species, and suffering among those least responsible for the problem. It may also be representative in terms of church involvement, given the accelerating engagement of faith groups on climate issues.

The Urgency of the Climate Challenge

Faced with an immediate threat to their own survival, Lateuans acted on a problem that is difficult for most humans to grasp. Climate change is a slow-motion danger whose advance is measured in years rather than hours or days, which makes it difficult for humans to perceive and take seriously—unless the waves are knocking at your door. But climate change is an urgent matter for all of humanity—arguably the most urgent environmental problem we face—for several reasons. Climate change:

- *is global in scope*. It is altering systems worldwide—from agriculture to water cycles to disease patterns—that have a direct bearing on the quality of our lives, and for many, a direct bearing on their prospects for survival.
- *has the capacity to remake human civilizations*. Scientists fear, for example, that melting ice from Greenland and the North Pole could pour enough fresh water into the Atlantic Ocean to shut down the Gulf Stream and its moderating impact on European temperatures, sending Europe into a new ice age.

- *brings a cascade of difficult-to-predict effects.* Warmer temperatures have emboldened the white pine beetle to migrate from the United States northward into Canada, where it is devastating forests. This has led loggers to cut huge stands of trees before they are infested, which in turn has prompted sawmills to operate around the clock.
- *is occurring faster than predicted.* Many scientists were alarmed in 2004 and 2005 at the rate of ice melt at both poles and in the world's alpine regions.
- *could soon become irreversible.* Some scientists argue that we have a decade or so to reduce greenhouse gases dramatically; otherwise the higher temperatures and the resulting changed planet could be locked in indefinitely.

But if climate change sounds like an abstract and distant environmental challenge, consider some of the unusual climatic events that have already taken place, and the toll they have taken on people, especially the poor:

- Hurricane Mitch parked itself over Central America in 1998, destroying huge swaths of infrastructure in Honduras and Nicaragua. *Some 9,000 people died.*[9] Economic losses were equal to 70 percent of GDP in Honduras, 45 percent in Nicaragua.[10]
- Extreme flooding afflicted China in 1998, displacing 14 million people and *affecting some 240 million people,* a number approaching the total population of the United States.[11]
- In the summer of 2004, two-thirds of Bangladesh and much of the Indian states of Assam and Bihar were under water after torrential rains. *More than 50 million people* were affected.[12]
- Floods in Mozambique in 2000 were *the worst in 150 years,* with water standing for months and destroying crops, food stocks, and seed reserves.[13]
- In the Sahel over the past 30 years, rainfall has decreased by 25 percent. By 1999, international aid agencies were supplying 1.7 million people in Kenya with emergency food, and by the summer of 2004 the number had climbed to *2.2 million people.*[14]
- Unusually warm weather in Europe in the summer of 2003 *killed tens of thousands of* people, mostly elderly, suggesting that while

climate extremes may afflict the poor the most, those in wealthy countries are not immune to climate catastrophes.[15]

While scientists are careful to point out that no single weather event can be attributed to climate change with certainty, these tragedies are consistent with climate models that predict higher temperatures and more frequent and intense storms. And by most scientific reckoning, more climatic instability and more suffering is humanity's fate unless action to stem climate change is taken urgently. Against this backdrop, religious groups are weighing in—especially Christians and Jews, who are influential in nations that are largely responsible for the climate problem. This is happening at various levels, from global policymaking to U.S. national and grassroots politics.

Global Activism

The World Council of Churches (WCC), which represents most Christian churches globally (with the exception of the Roman Catholic Church and some evangelical Christian churches), has pushed for a response to climate change since 1988, relatively early in the scientific debate about climate and well before global warming was an issue in the public mind. The work has been an uphill battle: carbon dioxide (CO_2) emissions continue largely upward, the number of people suffering from extreme weather events is on the rise, and the largest carbon-emitting country, the United States, seems largely oblivious to the problem, despite entreaties for engagement on the issue.[16] Despite the odds, David Hallman, coordinator of the WCC's Climate Change program, says the group "has no choice" but to be involved. "It's our ethical imperative."[17]

Actually, Hallman is quick to point to progress in religious involvement on climate, citing the "exponential growth" of faith communities engaged on the issue. As an example, he cites the unprecedented turnout of religious people at the 11th Conference of the Parties (COP) of signatories to the Kyoto Protocol in Montreal, Canada, in late 2005. More than 80 people were accredited to the conference under the auspices of the WCC, and another 10–15 faith representatives attended under the auspices of U.S. environmental organizations.[18] The group brought a strong and high-profile religious perspective to the meetings, drawing on uniquely religious strengths to make an impact on delegates.

One contribution was a large interreligious service entitled "Un cri de la Terre/Call of the Earth" held at St. Joseph's Oratory, a cathedral in Montreal. Some 1,500–2,000 people from the conference and local faith communities were present, and a wide range of traditions were part of the service. A native elder of a Canadian aboriginal group opened the gathering, and dance troupes from the Bahá'í, Christian, and Hindu traditions all performed. Climate witnesses from Fiji, India, Morocco, and the Arctic testified to the impact of climate change on their regions. Music and audio presentations were elaborate, including the ringing of a gong from Asia and the blowing of a shofar (horn) from the Jewish tradition.

Perhaps most significantly, attendees adopted "A Spiritual Declaration on Climate Change," which expresses religious concern about our warming planet.[19] (See Sidebar 6–1, p. 90.) The purpose of the declaration was twofold: It was presented to the conference itself as an input to deliberations and to political leaders, and it was presented to religious leaders from Bahá'í, Buddhist, Christian, Jewish, Muslim, and Hindu faith communities as a way of encouraging them to support local congregation efforts to address climate change.[20]

The WCC, along with several other non-governmental organizations (NGOs), was invited by the U.N. organizers to make a statement during the Ministerial High-Level Segment of the COP. The organizers regularly ask the WCC at these annual U.N. conferences to address the negotiators because they seem to count on the WCC to deliver an ethical, respectful, and strong message about the urgency of climate change from a justice perspective. As part of the presentation, Hallman called on Frances Noumoumou from Fiji to testify to the impact of a changing climate on her region and its communities, as a way of grounding the abstractions of climate change in the real world.

In addition to its interest in international policymaking on climate, WCC's climate work is broadening to include helping vulnerable peoples—like the people of Vanuatu, or, on a much larger

SIDEBAR 6–1. A Spiritual Declaration on Climate Change

The following declaration was issued by faith community participants during the United Nations Climate Change Conference, at a gathering at St. Joseph's Oratory, Montreal, on December 4, 2005.

We hear the call of the Earth.

We believe that caring for life on Earth is a spiritual commitment.

People and other species have the right to life unthreatened by human greed and destructiveness.

Pollution, particularly from the energy-intensive wealthy industrialised countries, is warming the atmosphere. A warmer atmosphere is leading to major climate changes. The poor and vulnerable in the world and future generations will suffer the most.

We commit ourselves to help reduce the threat of climate change through actions in our own lives, pressure on governments and industries and standing in solidarity with those most affected by climate change.

We pray for spiritual support in responding to the call of the Earth.

Source: See Endnote 19 for Chapter 6.

scale, the people of Bangladesh—adapt to climate change. The 2002 *World Disasters Report* noted that the number of reported disasters increased nearly threefold between the 1970s and the 1990s, from 1,110 to 2,742, and that many of these were related to the vagaries of a changing climate.[21] In the South Pacific, the number of people affected by disaster has increased some 65-fold in the last 30 years, even though population has not even doubled.[22] WCC has sponsored conferences in South Pacific nations to educate people about climate issues and to help them develop strategies for coping with their changing world.

Hallman sees the adaptation work as a natural for WCC, given its longstanding solidarity with the poor and vulnerable. He also sees the nitty-gritty adaptation initiatives and international policymaking work as being linked by inequity, a longstanding concern at WCC. Climate change, after all, is caused largely by wealthy industrial nations, yet the impact is found disproportionately in poor developing countries. Thus, WCC's "moral imperative" to engage the climate issue is threefold: it is a question of siding with suffering people, protecting the environment, and addressing a fundamental question of global fairness.

Not surprisingly, Hallman comes to his work from a concern for justice, one of two spiritual motivations he names as drivers of his work. The other, which he mentions first—perhaps surprisingly for such a grim topic—is joy. "I experience joy in life, in being able to participate in this incredible created Earth with its abundance and its incredible relationships, both human and non-human," he explains. "It seems incumbent on me to ensure that others are able to experience the same kind of joy that I do."[23]

An Emerging Climate Constituency: Christian Evangelicals

The human dimension to climate change may have made it easier to attract the attention of evangelical Christians in the United States, a group with substantial political clout in Washington. Perhaps best known for their strong stands against abortion, gay marriage, and other hot-button social issues, evangelicals also have longstanding concern for the poor, a key theme in the biblical texts on which evangelicals build their faith life. Some of the strongest voices protesting genocide in Darfur, Sudan, for example, are those of evangelical Christians. They are also vocal on the HIV/AIDS epidemic and sex trafficking in Africa. To be fair, some evangelicals have also taken leadership positions on "nature" issues, as the Evangelical Environmental Network's efforts to protect the U.S. Endangered Species Act demonstrate.[24] But the human dimension of climate change likely made it easier to enlist a broader evangelical constituency on climate change.

Indeed, the "conversion" of leading evangelicals has gathered steam quickly since 2000 as the current and potential human toll become more evident.[25] (See Table 6–1, pp. 92–93.) In February 2006, a virtual Who's Who of 89 evangelical leaders signed a document entitled

TABLE 6–1. The Evangelical Road to Commitment on Climate

Early evangelical activism on climate, 1990s

Calvin DeWitt, professor of environmental studies at the University of Wisconsin, founds the Evangelical Environmental Network (EEN) in 1993. EEN works to raise the profile of environmental issues, including climate change, among evangelicals. In 1994, it releases "An Evangelical Declaration on the Care of Creation," signed by more than 100 evangelicals. In 1995, EEN weighs in to support renewal of the U.S. Endangered Species Act.

Forum 2002, Oxford, U.K.

More than 70 scientists and religious leaders, including prominent U.S. evangelicals, meet to discuss climate change. They issue the Oxford Declaration on Global Warming, which states that human-induced climate change is a "moral, ethical, and religious issue" and calls for urgent action by Christian churches to raise awareness on climate and to prompt businesses and governments to adopt climate-friendly technologies and policies.

What Would Jesus Drive? campaign, 2003

EEN-run initiative challenges people to consider the environmental impact of their choice of car, drawing on climate-related arguments. EEN Executive Director Reverend Jim Ball drives a hybrid vehicle from Texas to Washington, D.C., stopping at churches and media centers to raise public awareness of the campaign.

Sandy Cove Conference, Maryland, 2004

EEN brings together a broad spectrum of evangelicals, from environmentalist Cal DeWitt to the leadership of the National Association of Evangelicals and representatives of Christianity Today. The more conservative attendees "would not have come in the 1990s," says Ball. Sir John Houghton, former co-chair of the Scientific Assessment Working Group of the Intergovernmental Panel on Climate Change in the 1990s as well as a committed evangelical, speaks about the need to respond to the climate crisis. Conference produces the Sandy

TABLE **6–1.** CONTINUED

Cove Covenant, which calls on evangelicals to engage "the most pressing environmental issues of our day," including climate change.

NAE Call to Social Action, 2004
National Association of Evangelicals (NAE) produces "For the Health of the Nation: An Evangelical Call to Civic Responsibility," a document that urges evangelical action on a series of public issues. "Creation Care" is among the top seven priorities.

ECI Call to Action, 2006
The Evangelical Climate Initiative (ECI) issues "Climate Change: An Evangelical Call to Action," signed by 86 high-profile evangelical leaders. The document asserts that Christian morality "demands a response" to the climate issue. It is not endorsed by the NAE, but more than a third of the signatories are NAE board or executive committee members.

Source: See Endnote 25 for Chapter 6.

"Climate Change: An Evangelical Call to Action," in which the plight of the poor emerges as a prime justification for engaging the climate issue. The 1,600-word statement contains one bolded sentence: "Millions of people could die in this century because of climate change, most of them our poorest global neighbors."[26] The document is hard-hitting, declaring that climate change is real, that the poor will be hit the hardest, that Christian morality demands a response, and that this response is needed now.

The statement's signers, who declare that "we are in the public square" of climate policy and "we will not withdraw," are all prominent figures in the evangelical community. They include the presidents of more than two dozen Christian colleges and universities, the editors of *Christianity Today* and *Sojourners* magazines, the CEO of National Religious Broadcasters, the author of the runaway Christian bestseller *The Purpose-Driven Life*, the head of the Salvation Army, the heads of several global relief agencies, including World Vision and World Relief, and the leaders of the Evangelical Environmental Network and Evangelicals for Social Action.

But there are key omissions to this group that suggest a major political battle may be brewing. James Dobson, president of Focus on the Family, Charles Colson of Prison Ministries Fellowship, and Richard Roberts, president of Oral Roberts University, are leading evangelical conservatives who argue there is enough uncertainty on climate questions that evangelicals should stay out of the debate. They formally asked that the National Association of Evangelicals (NAE), which represents some 30 million evangelicals from all 51 evangelical denominations in the United States, not endorse the statement.[27]

The conservatives prevailed. Indeed, they persuaded two important evangelical converts to the climate cause, NAE president Ted Haggard and vice president for governmental affairs Richard Cizik, not to join. Although fully convinced of the importance of the climate issue, Haggard and Cizik felt that signing would appear to give the NAE's endorsement to the document, which could destroy the fragile coalition of conservative and activist evangelicals, weakening evangelical influence in Congress and at the White House. Unity is a key source of evangelical strength but a difficult thing to maintain, given the reputation of evangelicals, as individuals and as individual churches, for fierce independence. Still, the climate activists may have momentum on their side: 34 of the 89 "Call to Action" signatories are on the Board or the Executive Committee of the NAE. If the evidence of a changing climate continues to tumble forth, it is quite possible that a strong majority of evangelical leaders and faithful will be converted to the cause of climate protection.

Religious Grassroots Activism

Climate is stirring people in the pews as well, a good example being the Interfaith Climate and Energy Campaigns in the United States, spearheaded by the National Council of Churches (NCC) and the Coalition on the Environment and Jewish Life (COEJL). The campaigns are organized by state—sometimes in coal, oil, or automobile producing states—and each works to educate religious leaders and congregations on climate issues and the Judeo-Christian religious teachings to care for all of creation. "In Genesis, God places Adam—adamah or earth—in the Garden of Eden...to serve and protect," says campaign program director Matthew Anderson-Stembridge. "Humans do have a special role in God's creation. We are called to be the serving and protecting inhabitants of God's creation."[28]

The potential for impact is large: Anderson-Stembridge notes that between the two organizations, NCC and COEJL, some 45–55 million Americans are represented. Getting just 1 percent of these people engaged on the issue, he says—some 500,000 people—could be politically powerful. "We want to convert this tremendous potential energy of faith into kinetic energy of ministry and witness," Anderson-Stembridge explains.[29]

Anderson-Stembridge's office coordinates the state efforts, offering training at annual meetings of state leaders and rallying the state organizations to meet national goals. In 2001, for example, the campaign persuaded more than 1,200 Protestant, Catholic, Jewish, and Muslim religious leaders from all 50 states to sign an open letter to Congress asking for specific measures, including stricter fuel efficiency standards, blocking oil drilling in a pristine area of Alaska, investment in renewable energy, and regulating CO_2 emissions from power plants.[30] Little progress has been made on the issue, but the stand is yet another notice from a religious quarter that religious people increasingly see climate as a priority issue.

Defending the Climate in Coal Country

The Interfaith Climate Change Campaign picked a formidable battleground when it set up shop in Pennsylvania. A major U.S. coal producing and consuming state, Pennsylvania trails only California and Texas in its emissions of the greenhouse gases that cause global warming. And as a major polluting state in a major polluting country—the state has five of America's ten dirtiest power plants—Pennsylvania is a global player in greenhouse gas emissions. Indeed, the average Pennsylvanian emits about five times more carbon dioxide and other greenhouse gases each year than the average person worldwide does.[31] And Pennsylvania's emissions alone are greater than the emissions from 105 developing countries *combined.*[32]

In this context, activism on climate issues in Pennsylvania could make a real difference. For Joy Bergey, the head of the Pennsylvania Interfaith Climate Change Campaign (PICCC) since early 2002, the challenge was literally a religious calling. A management consultant who founded and ran her own successful business, Bergey had been wrestling with a growing interest in her faith, on one hand, and her commitment to a healthy environment, on the other, neither of which was fed by her professional work. When a verse from Jeremiah rang out at an Ash Wednesday service in 2001—*Break up your fallow ground,* it said—Bergey heard a personal call. "It told me to change careers," she explains. "I knew it was addressed to me. It was really scary, but I felt I had to take the message to heart and heed the call."[33]

Bergey left her consulting business to lead the campaign in Pennsylvania, taking a huge pay cut. She has had to draw down her retirement savings to make ends meet, but declares emphatically, "I wouldn't trade it for the world." Successes in her new job appear to have compensated for the loss in income.

In 2004, Pennsylvania became the 19th state in the United States—and one of the few coal-producing states—to adopt a renewable portfolio standard (RPS), which requires that a certain share of a state's electricity be derived from wind, solar, geothermal, or other renewable energy sources. (In Pennsylvania, the RPS is called an Alternative Energy Portfolio Standard, or AEPS.) But the coalition that pushed it, including the PICCC, had to think creatively to achieve this in a state dominated by coal. They produced a two-tier system to govern energy use: on the one hand, the AEPS calls for greater use of wind, solar, and other renewable energy sources. But the second tier calls for a set of more controversial energy sources and strategies, from municipal solid waste, large-scale hydro, and conservation measures to burning slag piles of waste coal—a provision that angered many environmentalists. Yet without the provision for waste coal, the legislation would never have emerged from the state legislature.

Despite the compromise, PICCC reports that the AEPS will increase by eightfold the amount of clean energy generated by the state.[34] The AEPS will produce enough new wind energy for more than 1 million homes, or about 20 percent of all Pennsylvania homes.

And the solar power required by the AEPS is 0.5 percent, among the largest solar requirements in the country.[35]

Although progress on Pennsylvania's AEPS was the product of a coalition of secular and religious organizations, involvement of the latter made a unique difference. Bergey recounts that at one point, the state's secretary for the Department of Environmental Protection, Katie McGinty, knowing that the AEPS legislation needed help in the statehouse, made 250 copies of an op-ed written by the PICCC and submitted by the Pennsylvania Council of Churches outlining the religious argument for climate protection. She distributed these to legislators and their staff, with the cover note, "Look who is in favor of this." Bergey believes the tactic helped the legislation survive.

PICCC also had some success in prompting the state legislature to adopt a global warming plan of action. Bergey worked hard, through multiple phone calls, to persuade state Representative Bill Adolph, the Republican chair of the House Environment Committee, to meet with three constituents on the issue, including a Catholic priest. (Adolph himself is Catholic.) Adolph's response to the climate briefing, according to Bergey: "I had no idea the faith community was interested" in the issue.[36] When Bergey and her delegation asked Adolph to hold hearings on climate change and on the possibility of state adoption of a global warming action plan, he agreed and invited two scientists and Bergey to testify. A state climate plan is still a ways off, but Bergey believes that a strong showing by the state's faith community would substantially improve its chances.

Why does she do it? Bergey notes that, "My family is mostly conservative Republicans but we all love nature," a love she says dates back to her childhood. "Our vacations were often camping vacations, and I have always seen nature connected to God." She pauses reflectively: "(Nature) is a generous, sacred, irreplaceable gift to us."[37]

Rural Strategies for Climate Defense

For Anne D. (known to friends as Andy) Burt, a 61-year old Quaker grandmother who directs the Maine Council of Churches' Environmental Justice Program and its Interfaith Climate and Energy Initiative (ICEI), the motivation to become involved in climate work is deeply personal as well. "Ever since I became a grandmother six years ago, I have seen the Earth through a new set of lenses…. That my grand-daughter can't be in her home in Connecticut and know that polar bears are ok" is really troubling, says Burt, referring to the drumbeat of news about melting polar ice and the threat it poses to polar bears. But she is not defeated. "As I have learned more about climate change and the world she faces, it just spurs me on."[38]

As in Pennsylvania, the Maine program is strategically important for the prospects for climate action, in this case because Maine is represented in Congress by two moderate Republican senators. Persuading them of the need for action on climate could help move the governing party away from its disengagement on the issue.

ICEI got underway in 2000, at the same time that Maine Interfaith Power and Light was launched. The two groups worked together to build the market for green electricity in Maine, which at the time, according to Burt "was basically zero." Indeed, industry leaders told the groups that it would be too expensive to create and sustain interest in green energy in the state. But with their grassroots presence statewide, this is precisely what the churches were positioned to do. Over three years, 2,000 people signed letters of intent to join the project. Most were individuals, but some 30 churches—about 5 percent of the state's 580-member Maine Council of Churches—also committed, giving an early, institutional presence to the ICEI work.[39] Their success was especially noteworthy given that the green electricity option is more expensive in Maine. "There was a huge education curve for congregations," Burt says, because most don't look closely at their power use. "The people in a congregation who are interested in the environment are often not the people who hold the purse strings," she notes.[40]

Burt is also proud of the work of the program's Earth Care teams—basically the core of people from 50 or so congregations who are interested in environmental issues. These affiliate with the state program and undertake energy audits, educational campaigns, green energy, sales of compact fluorescent light bulbs, and other issues that each team deems appropriate for its congregation. Burt is impressed with the teams' energy and with the way they help each other with ideas and shared experiences. Their growing capacity to develop their own initiatives while collaborating with other congregations bodes well for engaging churches on environmental issues into the future, she says.[41]

Key to the program's operating strategy was to work with other groups and plug into relevant state programs. ICEI persuaded churches and synagogues, for example, to take advantage of the new governor's offer of free energy audits for small businesses, an important tool for identifying potential savings of energy—and cash. ICEI also engaged the state energy charter, which identified 54 measures that could lead to more efficient and more sustainable energy use. Burt and ICEI identified 10 measures that were particularly relevant for churches and focused members' attention on these, including: increasing congregations' levels of recycling; increasing the efficiency of heating and cooling systems and appliances; promoting locally grown produce; installing solar water heating and photovoltaics, using green builders and architects in renovations and new buildings; and participating in the governor's Carbon Challenge, which aims to reduce greenhouse gas emissions to below 1990 levels by 2010.[42]

Perhaps the most interesting characteristics of the Maine program were those that reflected the state's rural character. "It's hard to do a lot to bring public transport to people in a rural state," Burt notes. Instead, her group decided to focus on food and agriculture and their connection to energy and climate: "If people drive a shorter distance for their food and if they buy local food, it can have a climate impact." Moreover, because food and agriculture involve issues like hunger and justice—topics familiar to many churchgoers—the campaign could engage people on comfortable terrain. Burt reports that after leading a workshop at the state agricultural show, in which she made the connection between farmers and congregations, "a lot of the farmers came up to me and said that it felt right. It felt right to me, too, and when something feels right, you go with it. That's part of my Quaker experience." By focusing efforts on the unique strengths and needs of a rural state, the campaign could tackle traditional justice issues in Maine and make the climate connection at the same time.[43]

As with the energy audits, the program took advantage of opportunities already in place at the state level. Maine has a little-noticed Food Policy dating back to 1984, one of whose provisions is that Maine should be able to produce 80 percent of the calories consumed by all Mainers by 2020; today, the figure is about 40 percent, half of which is dairy. The policy also calls for increasing numbers of Maine households to purchase locally produced foods from Maine farmers, fishers, and food processors. ICEI is building programs that work to achieve these state goals. The programs include a "Be a Good Apple" covenant campaign, which asks people of faith to promise that $10 of their weekly food purchases will come from local sources. Participants cut off the tops of the pledge forms, which have the shape of an apple, and hang them on a tree to publicize the program and motivate congregation members. Burt reports that if every Maine household were to make this pledge, they could support all of the farm families in Maine—and reduce the carbon footprint of their food purchases.[44]

ICEI is also working to engage congregations in community supported agriculture (CSA), a scheme under which people contract with local farmers to receive vegetables and other produce over the course of the growing and harvesting season. But unlike most CSAs, which contract with individuals, Burt is working to get groups of congregants to sign on, and perhaps to have churches and synagogues be the drop-off point for the produce. She also has an eye on a "super CSA" model, which would supply not just the standard offerings of vegetables and flowers but also cheese, meat, bread, seafood, and other foods. Again, the benefits accrue not just to climate but to traditional areas of religious concern. Burt notes that CSAs can be a strong way to build communities, a religious value that may become more important as climate change and scarce energy increase the value of rooting our lives locally.[45]

Burt is excited about future activities, including a "climate witness tour" for the fall of 2006. The initiative would engage the Tuvalese Ambassador to the United Nations in a tour of congregations to show the movie "Trouble in Paradise: The Disappearance of Tuvalu," and to report on the effects of climate on his own people. It would also include a breakfast roundtable featuring people who can speak about climate change from different perspectives, including U.S. Senator Susan Collins, who has traveled to both the Arctic and Antarctica to see direct evidence of warming there.[46]

Burt is a grounded woman who lives in the woods and gets her electricity from solar cells. She is also deeply spiritual, and her thoughts on her work reflect her inner and outer selves. "We try to link creation of the physical world to our interior life. It's God within and God without," she explains. "How do we turn ourselves inside out—that's the challenge."[47]

Parisians take part in "The Incredible Picnic" on Bastille Day, 2000. The picnic ran down a meridien from the north to the south of France. An estimated four million people participated.

PART THREE

Progress
Re-Imagined

CHAPTER 7

New Vision: Choosing Well-Being

"Currently, success is measured by material advancements.
We need to readjust the definition of success to account for
time outside of work and satisfaction of life, not just the
dollars-and-cents bottom line."
—Betty Friedan[1]

Imagine that you're in charge of creating an economy. Think outside the box, perhaps by grappling with a few fundamental questions: What is an economy for? What should it do? What drives it? Who should run it?

To get your creative juices flowing, consider the experience of a small community on the plains of Colombia called Gaviotas. For 35 years, it has worked to create a different kind of economy, one with a strong emphasis on quality of life in harmony with the natural environment.

For starters, villagers ensure that basic needs are met: residents pay nothing for meals, medical care, education, and housing. All adults have work, whether in the various village enterprises that manufacture solar collectors and windmills, in organic and hydroponic agriculture, or in forestry initiatives. Social needs are addressed through the rhythm of daily activities: members work together in village businesses, and they often eat together in the large refectory while retaining the option to cook and eat in their own homes. Music and other cultural events are a regular part of village life.

With survival and social needs met in abundance, the atmosphere is peaceful: the community has had no police force, jail, or mayor in its 35-year history. Community norms are set by members and enforced through social pressure. And despite being in the middle of a country with an ongoing civil war, the community has been almost entirely untouched by it.

Gaviotas is no hippy haven for societal dropouts. It is a productive community known worldwide for its many inventions, including a water pump that village kids work as they ride their seesaw, windmills designed for the gentle breezes of the Colombian plains, a pressurized solar water heater, and a pedal-powered cassava grinder. Its air-cooled and solar-heated former hospital (now a water purification center) was named by a Japanese architectural journal as one of the 40 most important buildings *in the world*. The community's advances enhance the quality of life for Gaviotans, but also for other interested communities. As a matter of principle, the villagers do not patent their inventions, and indeed, make them widely available. Thousands of the windmills have been installed by Gaviotas technicians across Colombia, and the design has been copied throughout Latin America.

Villagers tread lightly on the environment, while using its resources to provide sustainable jobs and products. Gaviotas is self-sufficient in energy, through ample use of solar and wind power, methane produced from cattle manure, and biodiesel from the palm oil it cultivates. Its farming is organic. And it is the center of the largest reforestation project in Colombia, having converted more than 8,000 hectares of savannah to forest, from which villagers extract and sell only resin, even though logging would be more lucrative. Local rainfall has increased by some 10 percent since the planting of the forest, and the community has started bottling the water to sell in Bogotá.[2]

Think about what makes Gaviotas a standout community. Full employment. Little or no economic inequality. Basic needs satisfied. Economy in harmony with the environment. Personal security. Strong social interactions. Democratic governance. These diverse characteristics have one thing in common: they include most, if not all, of the characteristics that psychologists tell us are needed to make people happy. They are the ingredients for well-being.

Note, too, what is not part of the Gaviotas worldview. Maximization of profit. Privatization of knowledge. Growth at the expense of the environment. In most industrial societies today these are regarded as major engines of economic prosperity. Indeed, Gaviotas could be a wealthier community if it would only clearcut its forests and patent its inventions. But residents believe that greater wealth would ultimately come at the expense of quality of life.

That's the issue: wealth vs. well-being. The two are not mutually exclusive, of course: it's clear that wealth often expands people's options for well-being. But which goal is given the lead in an economy will strongly influence what the economy, and the community or society it supports, look like. A new vision of progress in the 21st century will require giving well-being the prominence and attention it lacked in the last century.

The Wealth Illusion

A major problem in industrial countries is the largely unquestioned assumption that greater wealth is the ticket to enhanced well-being. At some level we know the folly of this reasoning: the sage observation that "money cannot buy happiness" is now a cliché. The money-happiness disconnect in wealthy countries is clear when growth in income in industrial countries is plotted against levels of happiness. In the United States, for example, the average person's income more than doubled between 1957 and 2002 (with inflation factored out), yet the share of people reporting themselves to be "very happy" over that period remained flat.[3] (See Figure 7–1, p. 108.) And this truth is clear on the ground as well. Despite high and growing levels of per capita income in the United States between 1960 and the late 1990s, the divorce rate doubled, the teen suicide rate tripled, the prison population quintupled, and the number of people suffering from depression soared.[4]

Importantly, however, the relationship between wealth and life satisfaction is different in poor countries. There, income and well-being are indeed coupled, because more of a poor person's income is used to meet basic needs. Findings from the World Values Survey, a set of surveys of life satisfaction in more than 65 countries conducted

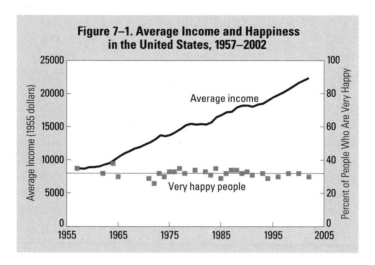

Figure 7–1. Average Income and Happiness in the United States, 1957–2002

between 1990 and 2000, indicate that income and happiness tend to track well until about $13,000 of annual income per person (in 1995 purchasing power parity). After that, additional income appears to yield only modest additions in self-reported happiness.[5] That is, money seems to help deliver happiness for people who are trying to cover life's basics, but at some point after those needs are met, additional wealth delivers less and less additional happiness.

Despite the evidence, governments of prosperous nations continue to chase economic growth with the single-mindedness of an addict. The idea that we might build economies that meet people's needs without perpetual increases in consumption is absent in most world capitals—and would be revolutionary if it did exist. Futurist Dennis Meadows observes that: "Some societies acknowledge that they would like their populations to stabilize. But there is no political system on earth that is striving for a stable material consumption for its people. Built into every political platform is the idea that it is good, and inevitable even, that material consumption is going to go up and up and up."[6]

We scramble for ever-greater wealth even when it no longer makes us happy, and indeed, even after it begins to harm the quality of our lives. The worldview holding this odd set of affairs in place—the beliefs that more is better, that new trumps used, and that we can never have too much, for example—has a powerful grip on the popular and official imagination. It will not be displaced easily, but will require something as powerful as an alternative worldview, well-being, to strip it of its legitimacy.

Well-Being as Genuine Wealth

Our understanding of well-being extends back at least half a century and continues to grow today. In 1954, the psychologist Abraham Maslow established a five-tier "hierarchy of human needs" that ranged from the concrete basics for survival such as food and shelter, to the more ethereal need for "self-actualization"—roughly, becoming the person one was born to be. Further research over the years on happiness and life satisfaction concluded that to achieve well-being, people generally need five things that echo Maslow's early findings: the basics for survival, good health, good social relations, security, and freedom.[7]

As knowledge regarding well-being has become firmer, the concept is gaining a modern, institutional following. The Canadian Parliament, for example, passed a motion in 2003 recommending that the government find ways to measure the well-being of Canadians.[8] The U.N.'s Millennium Ecosystem Assessment, which focuses on how ecosystem changes are affecting human well-being, uses a definition of well-being that is consistent with Maslow's hierarchy.[9] And researchers in the past 15 years have worked to develop alternative measures of societal progress that move beyond the blunt (though easy to grasp) GDP yardstick of total wealth. With growing agreement on the importance of well-being for humans, the potential to build economic activities on a foundation of human well-being, and not simply on wealth creation, would appear to be growing.

One effort to assess well-being, known as the Well-being Index, sums the measures of more than 80 diverse indicators, from life expectancy and school enrollment to deforested area and levels of carbon emissions, to produce scores on two major areas of progress, human well-being and ecological health. The approach is extremely useful: we can measure not only how well people in a country are doing, but the environmental price they pay for their prosperity. And we can compare the performances of the 180 countries it measures. The Index tells us, for example, that Sweden's prosperity is achieved relatively cleanly, while the Netherlands' nearly identical prosperity is substantially dirtier.[10] Tools like the Well-being Index help to measure the essence of sustainable progress: to improve people's lives with the least possible environmental impact.

The Look and Feel of Well-Being

In general, a well-being society would feature greater interaction among family, friends, and neighbors and more attention to finding fulfillment and creative expression than to accumulating goods. The goal would be to reduce the stresses—on people, communities, and the environment—that characterize life in many industrial societies today, and to achieve a deeper sense of life satisfaction than many people report experiencing today. Well-being has many dimensions involving individuals, communities, built infrastructure, and governments.

Individuals, for example, might opt to work less, as in Europe, where the number of people who voluntarily reduced their working hours grew by 5.3 percent annually between 1998 and 2003.[11] Many are also eating better: European organic agricultural area has increased some 60-fold since 1985 in response to consumer demand for organic food.[12] And a new market segment—"LOHAS" consumers, people who are interested in Lifestyles of Health and Sustainability—has appeared in the last decade, reflecting the desire of 63 million people to live in a healthier way.[13]

People pursuing a life of well-being often invest in relationships. Harvard Professor of Public Policy Robert Putnam has written that: "the single most common finding from a half century's research…is that happiness is best predicted by the breadth and depth of one's social connections."[14] Being socially connected has been shown to be good for one's health—the chance of dying in a given year, no matter the cause, is 2–5 times greater for isolated than for socially connected people—and for success in small businesses, where trust, reciprocity, and information networks grease the wheels of commerce.

Perhaps because of the appreciation of the importance of relationships, a modern form of village called "co-housing" is springing up in Denmark, the United States, Australia, and other industrial nations long criticized for the anonymity that characterizes life there. Co-housing involves 10–40 households grouped in a development that is designed to stimulate neighborly interaction. Privacy is valued and respected, but residents share key spaces, including a common dining hall, gardens, and recreational space. The communities are self-managed, which encourages interactions and sharing. Children typically have many adults watching as they play, as well as an abundance of playmates and babysitters. Most of the communities offer two or more common meals per week, with on average 58 percent of members attending.[15]

Well-being can be facilitated by good city and infrastructure design. Converting streets into pedestrian thoroughfares, mixing housing and shops, and creating plazas and parks, for example, can make city centers stimulating places that encourage civic interaction. And by building compact urban areas commuting times are curbed, saving workers one of the greatest assets for quality of life: time. In the United States, a suburbanite who spends an hour each day getting to and from work spends the equivalent of six workweeks in transit each year.[16] Businesses, too, can redesign their own physical infrastructure to cater to employee well-being. At the new Kansas headquarters of Sprint, a telecommunications firm, cars park at the edge of the corporate campus, and eating areas are some distance from offices, both of which require employees to walk during the day. Buildings feature slow elevators, which encourages people to use the stairs.[17]

Government policies can help foster a social environment of well-being in countless ways. It can also help people reclaim time. Belgium, Denmark, France, the Netherlands, and Norway now have 35- to 38-hour workweeks, which in addition to freeing up valuable time for workers often help to create new jobs. In the Netherlands, employers give the same benefits and promotion opportunities to part-time and full-time workers, making part-time work attractive for many, and the government encourages parents with small children to work the equivalent of no more than 1.5 jobs between them. Generous paid family leave—15 months of leave per child at up to 80 percent of salary—is the norm in Sweden.[18]

And serious government involvement of citizens in decision making can empower them to build communities of well-being. Officials in Porto Alegre, Brazil, have used a "participatory budget" process since 1989 to involve citizens directly in allocating the municipal budget, which has led to increases in the amount of money spent on education, basic services, and urban infrastructure—initiatives that have improved residents' quality of life. Most get involved by joining neighborhood meetings, so the process has helped to increase grassroots involvement, allowed new local leaders to emerge, and empowered some of Porto Alegre's poorer communities.[19]

Religious Interest in Creating Well-Being

Religions themselves have millennia of experience in creating Gaviotas-like communities of well-being, from Buddhist and Christian monasteries and religious communities to the kibbutzim of Israel. One village-based development movement in Sri Lanka with strong Buddhist values, known as Sarvodaya Shramadana, is now present in 15,000 villages—nearly two-thirds of the country's total of 24,000.[20] Well-being is reflected in the Sarvodayan vision of development, which is summarized in a list of 10 major human needs:

- a clean and beautiful environment
- a clean and adequate supply of water
- basic clothing
- a balanced diet
- a simple house to live in
- basic health care
- simple communications facilities
- basic energy requirements
- well-rounded education
- cultural and spiritual sustenance.[21]

Notice that nonmaterial assets such as a beautiful environment, well-rounded education, and cultural and spiritual sustenance are on par with material ones, suggesting that material and spiritual dimensions are both necessary for full development. In addition, the list yields a moderate but broadly based approach to consumption. Commodities are "basic," "simple," and "adequate," strongly communicating an ethic of sufficiency. In short, the list produces a materially narrower but spiritually broader understanding of healthy consumption than is found in modern industrial societies.

The Sarvodayan development goals also open up development opportunities more broadly across society. Modest use of resources saves them for use by others, thereby extending the reach of potential development efforts. And in an indirect way, the list serves as a quick-and-easy way to identify the individuals or groups most in need of further development assistance. This assessment would be a much more difficult task if the list were a long and virtually endless list of wants rather than a limited set of needs. The result is fulfillment of the Sarvodayan goal of "no poverty, no affluence."

Be Happy

In sum, a well-being society would approach the question of progress with a new set of priorities and yardsticks. It would be consistent with the wisdom of Enrique Peñalosa, the mayor who set out to remake Bogotá into a city of well-being. He was fond of commenting that "A city is successful not when it's rich, but when its people are happy."[22] (See Sidebar 7–1.) It would ask the fundamental question: why create economies that do not deliver what people ultimately want? Why not design them to deliver what makes people happy?

By nurturing relationships, facilitating healthy choices, learning to live in harmony with nature, and tending to the basic needs of all, societies can shift from an emphasis on consumption to an emphasis on well-being. This could be as great an achievement in the 21st century as the tremendous advances in opportunity, convenience, and comfort were in the 20th.

SIDEBAR 7–1. Bogotá: The Well-being Difference

Bogotá, the capital of Colombia, is commonly associated with civil war and violence. But in the late 1990s, the city's reputation began to change as Mayor Enrique Peñalosa led a campaign to improve the quality of life there. School enrollments increased by

200,000 students—some 34 percent—during Peñalosa's tenure. His administration built or totally rebuilt 1,243 parks—some small, some very large—which are now used by 1.5 million visitors annually. An effective rapid transit system, accessible to all, was planned and constructed. And the city's murder rate fell dramatically: today, there are fewer murders per capita in Bogotá than there are in Washington, D.C. By any standard, the city's advance is a developmental success. Yet Bogotá's transformation was achieved in a rather unorthodox way. When Peñalosa took office, consultants proposed building a $600-million elevated highway, a standard transportation solution in many car-bound cities. Instead, the mayor created a cheaper yet more effective rapid transit system using the city's existing bus lines. The system carries 780,000 passengers daily—more than the costlier Washington, D.C. subway does—and is so good that 15 percent of the regular riders are car owners.

Peñalosa also invested in hundreds of kilometers of bike paths and in pedestrian-only streets. And he strengthened the city's cultural infrastructure by building new public libraries and schools, connecting them with a network of 14,000 computers. Together with the rehabilitated parks, the transportation and cultural improvements advanced a strategic goal for Bogotá: to orient urban life around people and communities.

Source: See Endnote 22 for Chapter 7.

CHAPTER 8

Hungry for More:
The Consumption Challenge

*"Our enormously productive economy...demands that
we make consumption our way of life, that we convert the
buying and use of goods into rituals, that we seek our
spiritual satisfaction, our ego satisfaction, in consumption."*
—Victor Lebow[1]

The Old Order Amish, the devout, tight-knit communities of farmers and craftsmen in the eastern United States famous for their rejection of modern lifestyles, are commonly misunderstood. The stereotype is that they shun entirely modern conveniences such as cars and electricity in their effort to live simply.

But the truth is more complex, and more interesting: the Amish are not opposed to the use of technology, but are very careful about adopting it. They use electricity, for example, but only as much as can be coaxed from a 12-volt battery. Car transport is permitted, but only for rare and important trips, such as visits to the doctor. And a telephone may well be available, but typically in a common area accessible to a group of families, rather than in a private home. One writer calls the Amish "techno-selectives" who use technology in a bounded way that allows them to control their progress.[2]

The Amish process for circumscribing a technology is fascinating. A new advance—say, a cell phone—may be brought into an Amish community by one of its bolder, "early adopter" members. It is used over time, often for years, and perhaps picked up by others. All the while, people observe its use and think about it from the perspective of Amish values, especially whether it is increasing contact with the outside world, weakening ties within the community, or promoting a sense of pride among users, all of which are undesirable for the Amish. The talk of the community gets back to Amish bishops who eventually meet to discuss a single question: "Does this technology bring us together or draw us apart?"[3]

Thus, automobiles were found in some Amish communities until the 1960s, when bishops ruled against them after seeing that cars were taking members too far beyond community and family and jeopardizing their primary social ties. Telephones were deemed useful for emergencies and business use, but interrupted family life if placed in homes. Electricity was determined to be helpful, but if obtained from the municipal grid, would spur the adoption of appliances and promote an individualism and consumer pride that undermines humility. For all of these technologies, bishops said "Yes, but…," limiting their use in order to protect the web of community and family ties the faith values so dearly.[4]

The point is not to model the Amish lifestyle in its details, which are clearly more limiting than most people in industrial societies would accept today. Instead, the Amish gift to a culture of open-ended consumerism is this vital lesson: consumption is not an end in itself, but a tool that can help us to achieve personal or societal goals. Properly bounded, it can put us in charge of our progress—as the Amish clearly are of theirs.

A World Consumed

In contrast to the practice in Amish communities, goods and their use are clearly in the driver's seat among modern consumers. Consumerism is increasingly cited today as one of those great megatrends, like population growth or the spread of nuclear weaponry, weighty enough to affect the course of history. American historian Gary Cross, for example, asserts that the 20th century battle of the "isms" was won not by capitalism or socialism, but by "consumerism," so definitively has the drive to acquire and consume reorganized the lives of billions of people, peacefully and without coercion.[5] Canadian ecologist David Suzuki argues that consumerism has supplanted citizenship as the chief way that people participate in society.[6] Martin Luther King, Jr. once noted that the root problem in American society was not racism or imperialism or militarism, but materialism.[7] And interestingly for people of faith, some scholars now see consumption as the functional equivalent of a religion: millions live to consume, and see shopping and owning as the activities that most give meaning to their lives. One scholar, David Loy, has even called consumerism the first global religion.[8]

The comprehensive nature of consumerism means that it is not simply another in a laundry list of global sustainability issues. It is a meta-problem with ganglian ties to a host of other issues touching the planet and its people.[9] (See Sidebar 8–1, p. 118.) Nearly every environmental problem today can be linked to consumption to some degree, usually significantly. And high levels of consumption take a social and personal toll—from frayed social ties to poor health and even dampened levels of happiness—to the point that the quality of life of heavy consumers may actually be worse than the quality of life of people who consume more moderately. Because consumption spawns or influences so many other issues, it arguably ranks as the preeminent challenge to the effort to build a sustainable civilization.

Consumption is not a bad thing. People must consume to survive, and the world's poorest will need to consume more if they are to lead lives of dignity and opportunity. But consumption becomes consumerism when it becomes an end in itself—when it is an individual's primary goal in life, or the ultimate measure of the success of an economy. At that point, it threatens the quality of life of the prosperous and jeopardizes the development prospects of the poorest.

Religious Strength, Religious Silence

The fact that this chapter opens with a story of the Amish, rather than a mainstream religious group seeking to live simply, is ironic. The world's religions, including large, broadly accepted faiths, have more experience in teaching on consumption than on any other issue from the sustainability agenda. Most have warned, often for thousands of years, about the dangers of excessive attachment to

SIDEBAR 8–1. Three Worlds of Consumption

From a consumption perspective, the world can be divided into three parts, each of which manifests unsustainable patterns of consumption:

The wealthiest nations—In North America, Europe, Japan, Australia, and New Zealand, consumption is high and climbing. North America and Europe are home to 12 percent of the global population, but account for about 60 percent of global household expenditures. In these countries, consumption may be pursued for its own sake. Consider that the average new house in the United States in 2002 was 38 percent larger than the typical new house in 1975, when Americans were already living quite comfortably.

The prospering developing nations—In rapidly growing developing nations, including China and India, consumption is soaring, although modest compared with the richest nations. China, for example, had 7 million cell phone subscribers in 1996, but 350 million in 2005. In these countries, the challenge is not that people consume beyond a sustainable threshold, but that they are mimicking the fossil-fueled, waste-generating economic model of the industrial north.

The poorest nations—In parts of Asia, Africa, and Latin America, consumption is unsustainable because it is indisputably too low. Indeed, average household expenditures for sub-Saharan Africa were actually some 20 percent lower in 2000 than they were in 1980. A region already reeling from massive deprivation has seen its lot worsen within a generation.

Source: See Endnote 9 for Chapter 8.

material goods and wealth. And religions have credibility on the issue, as environmental writer Bill McKibben notes: "Among the institutions of our society, only the communities of faith can still posit some reason for human existence other than the constant accumulation of stuff." [10]

But aside from occasional statements from religious leadership about the perils of a consumerist lifestyle, and aside from the efforts of the occasional pioneering faith organizations (see Sidebar 8–2, p. 120), religious groups today do little to promote a simpler and fuller life.[11] Vows of poverty, intentional communities, and the experience of the Amish and Israeli kibbutzim stand as admirable examples of a more restrained relationship toward material goods. But these deal with a small subset of believers: priests and nuns, or those committed enough to devote their lives to a different way of living, such as the members of a kibbutz. Little effort is being made to spread the values and lessons of these groups to the larger religious populace.

If consumerism is the sustainability issue tailor-made for religions, it is also the issue on which the sustainability community needs the greatest help. The modern consumption problem—the purchase, use, and waste of resource-intensive stuff—appears to be intractable. Consumption trends in every consumerist society are up and rising steadily, even in societies like the United States that are already saturated with goods. And wealthy-nation levels of consumption leave little room for the majority poor of the world to stake their claims to a dignified life, given the many environmental thresholds that are already being crossed.[12] Consumerism in developed countries appears to have two speeds—fast and faster—and nobody has figured out how to slow this train before it creates an environmental and social wreck of historic proportions.

Consuming Differently vs. Consuming Less

One of the ways political and other leaders dodge the issue of reducing consumption is by changing the subject. To the degree that consumption is regarded as a problem, it is typically framed in terms of a need to consume more ethically, for example by purchasing fair-trade coffee, vegetables from local farmers, or energy-efficient light bulbs. As previous chapters have argued, these initiatives are all good, and should be vigorously promoted. But if they become a substitute for simpler living, they turn our attention away from one of the greatest ethical demands of our generation (and arguably, one of the greatest opportunities to reclaim rich, community-centered lives).

SIDEBAR 8–2. Selling Simplicity

Standing virtually alone at the crossroads of faith and consumption is an organization called Alternatives for Simple Living, located in the U.S. state of Iowa. For more than three decades, it has spread a religiously inspired message of simplicity. The organization is best known for its resources to help Christians recapture the essence of Christmas by celebrating the holiday more simply and meaningfully. But they also offer a variety of educational resources, enlist a group of 800 volunteers across the United States to help people or groups interested in living more simply, and offer workshops on living with less and on re-imagining holiday celebrations.

National Coordinator Gerald Iversen is not naïve about the challenge facing the organization. "The average citizen is exposed to 16,000 hits of advertising a day," he says, from subtle influences like a commercial jingle and logos like the Nike "swoosh" to full-blown print, radio, and TV ads. He likens the simplicity message to a gadfly: tiny and seemingly inconsequential, it is annoying enough to capture people's attention at least occasionally.

Iversen appreciates the irony that churches, with millennia-worth of teaching on the value of moderation, are largely inactive in addressing consumerism today. Houses of worship are part of the consumer system, he observes, because they depend on the wealth of their members for donations that allow them to run their programs. He also observes that consumerism is an addiction that is extremely difficult to break. And he notes that swimming against the consumerist tide is difficult. "Simple living is more than charity. It works for justice. That involves changing systems, including our own lifestyles."

Iversen believes that it will take a crisis, such as critically short energy supplies, to get people to simplify their lives. But he also notes that a small handful of people already live simply by choice, and that they experience a joy, freedom, and newfound time for relationships and other high-value priorities that make simplicity well worthwhile.

Source: See Endnote 11 for Chapter 8.

Our primary focus needs to be on the quantity of stuff consumed, and switching to ethically produced goods may do nothing to address the quantity issue.

A narrow focus on ethical consumption is problematic for two other reasons. First, ethical consumption alone cannot tackle the structural problems associated with consumption, such as a lack of public consumption choices relative to private ones. Consumer economies make huge quantities of goods available for private purchase: the tens of thousands of items in the average U.S. supermarket may well include more than 100 kinds, sizes, and brands of breakfast cereal. Compare this cornucopian choice with the paucity of goods available for public consumption: in many communities in high-consumption countries, it may not be possible to choose a high-quality school, a safe, bikable path to work, or a swimmable river. The problem with the imbalance in public and private choice sets, according to a report from the Fabian Society in the U.K., is that the expansive private choice sets tend to have a high environmental cost and tend to benefit the well-off. More ethical consumption by individuals, while laudable, does nothing to change this structural problem.[13]

And when ethical consumption means consuming more efficiently, the results may not be as helpful as expected. If I buy a car that gets 25 percent better gas mileage than my current one, it would seem that everyone is better off: I spend less on gas, the air is less polluted, and car dealers benefit from a new sale. But economists have documented a "rebound effect" from efficiency. People often respond to greater efficiency with greater consumption, offsetting some or all of the efficiency gains. Fuel-efficiency increases of American cars since the 1970s have been more than canceled by increased fuel use, for example.[14] And while energy and water use at the U.S. level, and materials use at the global level, have all become more efficient since 1970, total use of those resources is also up.[15]

The problem comes when efficiency becomes a substitute for conservation, argues Andy Rudin of the Philadelphia-based Interfaith Coalition on Energy. The distinction is important. Conservation means using less in an absolute sense—"turning things off," says Rudin—whereas efficiency is about using less per person, per square meter, or per kilometer. "I don't know of an instance where a person uses something less because it is more efficient," Rudin asserts.[16] He is a big fan of the Amish precisely because of their emphasis on conservation, which clearly trumps efficiency in their worldview.[17] He once calculated that it would be six times cheaper—and therefore, economically more efficient—for the Amish to get their electricity from the grid. But their emphasis on conservation is what gives the Amish a far lighter environmental footprint than their neighbors who use energy-efficient appliances and machines.

Rudin's counsel to congregations looking to save energy is first to conserve, then to buy renewable energy, and last, to purchase more-efficient machinery and appliances. Of course, the ideal would be to combine both conservation and efficiency, as Rudin himself does at home. "While Joyce and I own efficient appliances, lights, and boiler, we keep them off as much as possible."[18]

Too often, however, consumers and policymakers focus heavily on efficiency and hardly at all on conservation, because efficiency appears to be a painless way to address resource use. It is much easier and more fun to buy a new and more efficient washer, range, or car than it is to wash, cook, or drive less. But in a world whose economies regularly and increasingly overtax the natural environment, the failure of efficiency alone to put economies on a sustainable path suggests that leadership on conservation is sorely needed.

Absent an immediate crisis—a cutoff of oil supplies, for example—political leaders are unwilling to make the case for lowered consumption. And most business leaders still lack the imagination to conceive of a prosperous world of lessened consumption. The only leaders of any standing in most societies who might carry the message, as writer Bill McKibben has argued, are religious leaders. They, after all, can make the moral argument about humanity's responsibilities to the environment. But they can also speak from experience about the potential to build communities with a high quality of life through greater sharing and simpler lifestyles.

The Spiritual Dimension

The bishop of London, Richard Chartres, once noted that St. Francis, the 13th-century Tuscan advocate for the poor and lover of nature, came from a wealthy family and was, by the standards of his day, a heavy consumer. A conversion experience convinced him to abandon the life of nobility and embrace a bare-bones lifestyle as a pathway to God. Chartres sees a lesson for people of faith. "We move toward God by subtraction, rather than accumulation," he says, a consumption ethic embraced by many world religions.[19] (See Table 8–1, p. 124.)

At the core of each of these teachings is the concept of restraint. But what is the spiritual value of restraint? Franciscan writer and lecturer Richard Rohr notes that the work of spiritual growth usually happens when a person is in a psychological state of surrender, and this typically requires the kind of suffering we call self-denial. This is why fasting, retreats, and silence are common paths to spiritual growth in many religious traditions. "The bubble of order has to be broken," writes Rohr, "by deliberately walking in the opposite direction. Not eat instead of eat…. Silence instead of talking, emptiness instead of fullness." Rohr sees this embrace of suffering, which he defines as not being in control, as central to many religious traditions. "In the west we have called this transformation process salvation, the Jews might have called it passing over, Buddhists perhaps enlightenment, we Franciscans call it poverty, but the Eastern church has most daringly…called it divinization."[20]

The engine at the heart of modern industrial economies is of course markedly different in character. The promise of happiness and fulfillment in television ads is found not in restraint but in unlimited indulgence. Advertising tells us that we can "have it all," that we deserve more, that no payments are required for 18 months. Indeed, it is hard to imagine a television ad inviting us to not acquire, to quiet down, to not compete, to simply listen. The modern promise of limitless choice, Rohr argues, is spiritually stultifying: "'I choose, therefore I am' creates self-absorption and narcissism," he writes. "'I am chosen, and therefore I am,' creates saints and mystics."[21]

TABLE 8–1. Selected Religious Perspectives on Consumption

Faith	Perspective
Bahá'í Faith	"In all matters moderation is desirable. If a thing is carried to excess, it will prove a source of evil." (Baha'u'llah, Tablets of Baha'u'llah)
Buddhism	"Whoever in this world overcomes his selfish cravings, his sorrows fall away from him, like drops of water from a lotus flower." (Dhammapada, 336)
Christianity	"No one can be the slave of two masters.... You cannot be the slave both of God and money." (Matthew, 6:24)
Confucianism	"Excess and deficiency are equally at fault." (Confucius, XI.15)
Daoism	"He who knows he has enough is rich." (Dao De Jing)
Hinduism	"That person who lives completely free from desires, without longing...attains peace." (Bhagavad-Gita, II.71)
Islam	"Eat and drink, but waste not by excess: He loves not the excessive." (Q'uran, 7.31)
Judaism	"Give me neither poverty nor riches." (Proverbs, 30:8)

Source: See Endnote 19 for Chapter 8.

A Question of Solidarity

Many religious traditions stress the need to care for the poor, an ethical imperative with a direct relationship to consumption: deprivation becomes morally scandalous in a world of great wealth. Yet this is the reality today. The United States, Canada, Australia, Japan, and Western Europe—with among them 15 percent of the world's population—use half or more of the key resources such as aluminum, lead, copper, and steel.[22] The United States alone, with less than 5 percent of the global population, uses about a quarter of the world's fossil fuel resources.[23] And although income inequality has improved slightly as India and China have prospered, the long-term trend has been gloomy: the World Bank estimates that inequality among the world's nations doubled between 1820 and 1990, and that inequality within nations has generally worsened as well.[24]

But what cinches the argument that consumption is a moral issue is that so little sacrifice on the part of the wealthy is needed to make a difference for the poorest. Vaclav Smil, in his book *Energy at the Crossroads*, notes that a reduction in energy use in wealthy countries of 25–35 percent "would call for nothing more than a return to levels that prevailed just a decade or no more than a generation ago. How could one even use the term sacrifice in this connection? Did we live so unbearably 10 or 30 years ago that the return to those consumption levels cannot be even publicly contemplated by serious policymakers?"[25]

Indeed, in 1973, authorities in Los Angeles feared that the Arab oil embargo would leave the city far short of the oil it needed, and asked citizens and businesses to cut their energy use by 12 percent, authorizing fines for those who did not comply. Households and businesses could meet the goals any way they preferred. In the end, no fines were levied: the cutback in energy use was 17 percent, without any closed business or other apparent hardship. The Dodgers baseball team met its target reduction by moving the starting time for games from 8 p.m. to 7:30 p.m.[26] The padding in Angelenos' consumption habits apparently was so great that large cuts were possible with virtually no pain.

If anything, the slack available to help the poor is greater than ever. Table 8–2, on page 126, shows the levels of investment needed to provide some of the basics for a dignified life, and compares these with the quantities spent on various luxury goods and services in wealthy countries.[27] Providing adequate food, clean water, and basic education for the world's poorest, for example, could all be achieved for less than people spent annually on makeup, ice cream, and pet food in 2000. The point is not to condemn wealthy countries for enjoying life; reasonable people may well disagree about the point at which

TABLE 8–2. Annual Expenditure on Luxury Items Compared with Funding Needed to Meet Selected Basic Needs

Product	Annual Expenditure	Social or Economic Goal	Additional Annual Investment Needed to Achieve Goal
Makeup	$18 billion	Reproductive health care for all women	$12 billion
Pet food in Europe and U.S.	$17 billion	Elimination of hunger and malnutrition	$19 billion
Perfumes	$15 billion	Universal literacy	$5 billion
Ocean cruises	$14 billion	Clean drinking water for all	$10 billion
Ice cream in Europe	$11 billion	Immunizing every child	$1.3 billion

Source: See Endnote 27 for Chapter 8.

consumption becomes "excessive." Instead, the analysis demonstrates the level of surplus wealth found in the most prosperous countries, and implicitly poses a question: why does chronic suffering continue, when a bit more sharing would be so painless for the wealthy, and so beneficial for the poor?

Seeds of Activity

Given the spiritual and moral case to be made for reduced consumption, the striking reality is how little activity on the issue is under way. The smattering of small-scale examples from an Internet search suggest that a few people, largely isolated from each other, are courageously taking a stand against what seem to be impossible odds, but that their impact society-wide is yet to be felt. The Archbishop of Canterbury, Rowan Williams, has written a book criticizing "rampant consumerism," particularly because of its impact on children.[28] The movement for a TV-free week, started in the United States but now spreading internationally, is attracting some religious support among Christians and Jews concerned about the effect of ads and programming on their children.[29] And in December 2005, an evangelical group called the American Family Association appealed for a ban on Christ-mas gifts.[30] In this last example, the call was supported by the Net-work of Spiritual Progressives, a collection of people of many faiths with left-leaning politics, founded by Rabbi Michael Lerner (suggest-ing that moderating consumption could be an area on which con-servative and liberal religious people might work together).[31] Admirable as these efforts are, they stand out as much for their novelty as for their nobility.

CHAPTER 9

Mindful Investments

"They who give have all things; they who withhold have nothing."
—Hindu Proverb[1]

Observe customers leaving the One World Shop in Glasgow with fair-trade furniture, hand-woven rugs, wooden toys, musical instruments, and exotic coffees, and you are witnessing the tip of an economy of well-being. Shoppers at this all-fair-trade store leverage their consumer spending in favor of poor producers, by agreeing to pay higher-than-world-market prices for their goods, a premium that is passed along to the farmers, craftspeople, and small manufacturers in Africa, Asia, and Latin America. Customers can be assured that their purchases touch many lives: business manager Rachel Farey estimates that her store alone stocks the wares of roughly 5,000 producers in developing countries. The shop is the visible piece of a burgeoning movement: fair trade sales in Europe, for example, are up more than 20 percent annually since 2000.[2]

But beneath the inspiring commerce at One World Shop is a second, even more powerful story, a tale of ethically-leveraged financial flows that grease the wheels of fair trade and help to explain its rapid growth. The Kuapa Kokoo Cooperative in Ghana that supplies the cocoa beans for One World's Divine Chocolate, for example, are financed through microcredit, small-scale financing that typically allows producers to obtain raw materials or other inputs needed for production. Financing to pay suppliers in Bangladesh for jute shopping bags, in India for leather wallets and purses, and in Vietnam for silk handbags came from a company called Shared Interests, which provides credit exclusively for fair trade products. And the Glasgow shop itself would not exist without the help of Charity Bank, an institution that lends exclusively to small organizations, often nonprofits, that cannot qualify for a commercial loan.

Financing in all three cases—for the goods, for the trade, and for the shop itself—came from institutions that make capital available to sectors that cannot normally get it. And in all three cases, the capital for these financial institutions came from investors, often religious people and institutions, who wanted to leverage their investments for good. Through these investment opportunities, they were able to put their wealth to work far beyond the impact of their ethical purchases and charitable donations.

Rachel Farey is proud of the difference her store is making in people's lives. Last year, she met the women from Bangladesh who produce jute shopping bags for One World Shop—colorful, woven satchels with screen print designs on the front—and learned that they recently had electricity installed in their homes for the first time, thanks to their sales to One World.[3] She has also met the cocoa farmers who supply the ingredients for the store's chocolate, and learned that their village had just dug its first well, eliminating the daily ten-kilometer walk to fetch water from the river.[4] The experience of these producers is moving evidence that the choices of ethical consumers, supported by an underlying web of ethical investing, is creating well-being transactions—pieces of what could someday be well-being economies—in which wealth is a tool, rather than an end, and where prosperity is more broadly shared.

Treasure Abundant

Most of the world's religions place great value on generosity, particularly in service of the poor and marginalized in society. And by many measures, religious people are generous: their contributions to houses of worship and associated programs accounted for 60 percent of all charitable giving in the United States in 2000.[5] Add to this their contributions to secular organizations, and it is clear that religious people have an outsized presence in the world of charity.[6] Total giving to religious charities in 2004 (presumably by religious people) amounted to more than $88 billion.[7] But religious charitable giving is like fair-trade purchases: while greatly needed and highly commendable, it only begins to tap the potential power of religious wealth for good. Religious people's investable funds, not just the grants that constitute charitable donations, remain largely untapped. They could potentially be steered to create a more just and sustainable world, even as they remain in the name of the investor.

Institutions and religious individuals collectively hold huge stocks of wealth in the United States. To take one example, a Citigroup study has estimated the country's United Methodist Pension Fund to be worth $12 billion.[8] An impressive figure, it is nevertheless a trifle compared to the investing power of the six million or so Methodist families, whose cumulative investable wealth was estimated at between $250 billion and $500 billion.[9] That, in turn, is a pittance compared to the total investable wealth of all Christians in the United States. If the 31 percent of American Christians who attend church weekly own a proportionate share of the professionally managed funds in the United States, these regular churchgoers owned some $6.05 trillion in invested wealth in 2005.[10] (This estimate is conservative, because it counts only the wealth of Christians, and only those Christians who attend church weekly. It is especially conservative in light of the large share of Americans—60 percent—who gave to a religious organization in 2000.)

Individual and institutional religious investments (along with secular investments) are likely to expand substantially over the coming half-century as the greatest intergenerational transfer of wealth in history unfolds. Analysts estimate that between 1998 and 2052, at least $41 trillion will pass from aged parents to their children in the United States.[11] If 31 percent of this total goes proportionately to the American Christians that attend church regularly, another $10 trillion will be in the hands of regular churchgoers.[12] (Again, the estimate is conservative: if the 60 percent of generous Americans referred to above were to receive a proportionate share of the coming windfall, the total headed to people who are religious or sympathetic to religion would be nearly $25 trillion.) Much of this wealth will not be liquid—it will consist to a large degree of land and property—but will nevertheless offer huge new investment opportunities that can conceivably be used to help create societies of well-being.

Thus, with more investable capital than ever and with more coming, religious people in wealthy countries are in a strong position to steward their wealth by taking into account the needs of the larger world around them. Despite the potential, however, persuading religiously motivated investors to channel a share of their inheritance to investments in organizations without access to commercial capital will not be easy. Religious giving, as impressive as it is, may actually be falling compared with the potential.[13] (See Sidebar 9–1.) Reverend Terry Provance of Oikocredit, a nongovernmental organization that invests religious wealth in microenterprises in developing countries, observes that when it comes to their money, even

---

SIDEBAR 9–1. Religious Charity and Giving Potential

Although religious individuals in the United States give large sums to charity in absolute terms, the numbers are less impressive from at least one perspective. A research group called The Empty Tomb that tracks religious giving has shown that as a share of income, giving in the United States has generally fallen in recent decades, from 3.1 percent in 1968 to 2.6 percent in 2003. (Giving stood at 3.2 percent of income in 1933, when the U.S. was well into the Great Depression.)

The group also calculated that if religious Americans upped their giving to 10 percent of their income—the classic "tithe"—some $94 billion would be available each year for charitable and development work in the United States and abroad. This sum is more than the entire annual estimated cost, some $69 billion, for achieving the United Nations' Millennium Development Goals, which include objectives like cutting in half extreme poverty and hunger, providing universal primary education, promoting gender equality, reducing mortality rates for mothers and children, and reversing the spread of infectious diseases.

Source: See Endnote 13 for Chapter 9.

religious people get nervous about its disposition. "There's often a gap between the rhetoric of justice and investment values," he reports.[14] Anyone who has experienced the seductive power of wealth can understand this. But building economies of well-being may require a new outlook on wealth, one that measures returns on investment broadly, to include both financial and social returns.

Investing for Good

Fortunately, opportunities to leverage personal and institutional wealth are expanding rapidly under a set of investment options known as socially responsible investing (SRI). SRI typically involves three main areas of activity: screening investments for their environmental or social impact; pressuring for changes in corporate practices through the use of shareholder resolutions at corporate annual meetings; and investing in communities that are underserved by traditional financial institutions. Interest in ethical investment has grown rapidly in recent years: in the United States, socially responsible investment leapt more than 35-fold between 1984 and 2005, from $59 billion to some $2.01 trillion (in 2000 dollars).[15] In the United Kingdom, SRI got a later start, but grew tenfold between 1997 and 2001. Indeed, all major investing regions, including emerging markets in developing countries, are seeing increased demand for SRI options.[16]

Although the most rapid growth in SRI has occurred just since the late 1990s, the roots of ethical investment go back centuries, even millennia, to early religious counsel regarding the proper use of wealth. Perhaps not surprisingly, then, religious communities were particularly vocal in challenging investment patterns as corporations came into being and as stock markets began to emerge. Quakers and Methodists, for example, avoided investments that might have benefited the slave trade, and in 1928 the religiously-led Pioneer Fund was set up to avoid investments in alcohol, tobacco, gambling, and other "sin" businesses.[17] By the 1970s, religious communities began to coordinate efforts to advance responsible investment, which made them leaders in the SRI movement. Indeed, until very recently, religious groups were the predominant presence in SRI activity. In the U.K. in 1997, for example, religious holdings accounted for just over 50 percent of ethical investing activity, but by 2001, religions' share had dropped to just 5 percent as secular ethical investing exploded.[18]

Packing an Institutional Punch

The chief center of religious coordination on ethical investment for more than three decades has been the Interfaith Center on Corporate Responsibility (ICCR) in the United States. Today, it consists of 275 faith-based institutional investors with combined portfolios worth an estimated $110 billion.[19] The Center, whose members include religious communities, denominations, and dioceses, as well as city and state pension funds, unions, foundations, colleges, and healthcare corporations, works primarily to organize shareholder advocacy initiatives on behalf of religious institutional investors.

ICCR's activities are organized around nine working group areas that cover global warming, water and food, corporate governance, militarization, health care, access to capital, contract supplier standards, and human rights.[20] These focus areas can change every five years, as priority issues shift and as the context for business operations changes. ICCR member organizations sponsor or co-sponsor some two-thirds of the social issue resolutions presented at corporate shareholder meetings each year.[21]

The work requires persistent effort. ICCR has been engaged since 1993, for example, to pressure Wal-Mart, the world's largest retailer, on issues of worker dignity, including provision of health care and guarantee of a living wage to employees throughout the company's globally strung supply chain. The agenda is ambitious and long-term, but ICCR has seen some progress. In 1996, pressure from ICCR and other investors led Wal-Mart to take responsibility for labor conditions in the factories of its suppliers. In 2005, the company amended its supplier policy to address the right of workers to organize a union and to bargain collectively. And Wal-Mart now has a transparent policy on racial and gender diversity, thanks to shareholder pressure for it to release data on its personnel practices. ICCR sees more work ahead in the coming years, but is optimistic that the company will evolve into a firm "worthy of moral and financial investment."[22]

Another area of ambitious ICCR activity is climate change. Efforts here focus on encouraging companies to report their carbon footprints, inform shareholders of the risks and opportunities that climate change poses for the company, and reduce emissions of greenhouse gases. The group is now a partner in a campaign by Co-op America to encourage Vanguard, Fidelity, and American Funds—the three largest mutual fund companies in the United States, with 70 percent of mutual fund assets—to consider the climate-change impact of the companies they invest in.[23] None of the three companies, for example, voted for any climate-change-related shareholder resolution presented to companies in 2005.[24]

Few of the resolutions spearheaded by ICCR pass, and many receive support from less than 10 percent of shareholders. But passage of resolutions is not the proper measure of success. Sister Patricia Wolf, the group's executive director, notes that corporate leaders pay attention to even relatively small groups of disgruntled shareholders: as ICCR's success at gaining support for shareholder resolutions has increased over its 30 year history, so has the flow of visiting CEOs to her New York office. Today, she estimates, some 50 percent of her time is spent meeting with corporate executives, often from large companies like Ford, Apple, and Bristol-Myers Squibb, who are responding to resolutions. "Our work has changed," Sister Pat notes. "We are perceived as having great value in helping companies to shape their reports" so that they contain commitments to more responsible business practices.[25]

ICCR is influential not only in providing leadership on shareholder resolutions, but also because of the unique perspective it brings to many issues. The group draws corporate attention to HIV/AIDS and other issues that emerge from the grassroots work of religious communities. The poor typically don't have a voice in community affairs, but with a strong religious presence in many low-income areas of the United States and of the world, religious communities are in a position to advocate for the poor, and to use shareholder advocacy for this purpose.

Pooling Assets for Influence

One of the newest and potentially most influential institutions for leveraging religious wealth of all kinds is the International Interfaith

Investment Group, known formally by its more playful moniker, 3iG. Launched in 2005 after three years of organizing work sponsored by the Alliance of Religions and Conservation (ARC) of the U.K., 3iG is the first global-level effort to harness religious wealth for good. 3iG organizers intend for the new organization to increase the impact of religious wealth in three ways: by redirecting investments toward sustainable businesses; increasing religious presence at shareholder meetings, just as ICCR does; and encouraging the spread of ethical investment practices to individual congregants.[26]

At the inaugural launch of 3iG in April 2005, members spoke of the importance of moving beyond the "negative screens" that have characterized socially responsible investment since its inception. These screens offer ethical investors a way to avoid funding companies that manufacture arms, cigarettes, nuclear power technology, or other morally controversial goods or services. But negative screens are limited in their capacity to leverage wealth, because screens vary in rigor and, more importantly, because they do not steer investors toward companies whose work is in line with sustainable development. 3iG encourages its members to use what the Bishop of London, Richard Chartres, has called a "via positiva" approach to religious investing.[27] It asks institutions to apply their wealth proactively in ways that will help to create the better world they envision.

The "via positiva" approach may become a widespread option for investors, if research by the London-based financial firm Henderson Global Advisors is on the mark. Seeking a set of investments for the proactive ethical investor, the firm reorganized its ethical investment business into 10 categories of sustainability, from clean energy and sustainable transport to health and quality of life. The staff then asked themselves, "How many companies in the world have *as their core activity* the advancement of one or more of these areas of interest?" The idea was to identify firms whose work was largely consistent with sustainability, while taking care to avoid those—such as oil companies with a small solar division—that merely talk a good game. Across the 10 categories it found more than 7,000 companies involved in the work of "sustainability solutions," in Henderson's words. After eliminating inaccessible companies (those listed, for example, on a remote stock exchange), some 4,000 companies remained, from which Henderson selected those with the best investment prospects.[28]

The best news is that these companies are fully competitive with more traditional investment portfolios. Henderson's Industries of the Future fund, the result of its research, was launched in April 2005 and has performed at least as well as the Morgan Stanley Capital International (MSCI) index, a standard benchmark of portfolio performance.

Targeted Impact

3iG member institutions also influence religious investment through their capacity to identify a need for investments or shareholder activism on particular issues. Member institutions work together to identify high-priority "cluster" areas—the inaugural ones are water, forests, microfinance, and labor dignity—and communicate these to the 3iG membership at large.

One illustration of how 3iG-led investments could work is found in a reforestation project in Mozambique, spearheaded by the Västeras diocese of the Church of Sweden. The project centers on a 90,000-hectare stretch of land in Västeras' sister diocese of Niassa, an area that has been deforested to the point of barrenness, in part because of local need for charcoal as a fuel source. The Church will lead a group of investors, including the Church of Norway, the Anglican Church in the U.K., Harvard University, and some commercial banks, all organized under the 3iG banner, in providing $32 million over 10 years to reforest the area and generate income and jobs from it.[29]

Half of the reforested area will become a conservation reserve sown with native species. "The goal is to get the area to an ecologically pristine state" by restoring it to former, forested conditions, according to Asa Tham of the Church of Sweden and CEO of the Global Solidarity Fund, which is running the project.[30] The other half of the area will be used for plantation forestry that will produce sawn wood and chips for fuel from pine, teak, and eucalyptus plantations. Local communities are involved in project planning and will be allotted a share of the wood from the plantations. They will also be engaged to protect the forests from fire and illegal logging. Since the project's start in 2004, it has created 260 local jobs, with the potential to create 400.[31]

The effort is a natural fit for the Church of Sweden. On the one hand, the Church has a long history of involvement in forestry issues; it is the seventh largest landholder in the country, with huge tracts of forest, an artifact of the Middle Ages when local parishes were large landowners. The Church has worked to leverage this ownership for environmental good by placing 25 percent of its holdings under Forest Stewardship Council certification, which ensures that forests are managed according to principles of sustainability established by the Council.[32] At the same time, the Church has a longstanding interest in development projects in poorer countries, and in carrying these out in an environmentally sensitive way. This project meets both criteria.

The project is also a prudent use of the Church's wealth. Investors can expect—in addition to a clear conscience—a yield of 5 percent annually after Year 5, and 20 percent by Year 18. On a present value basis, returns will average 13 percent.[33]

Micro Loans for Macro Impact

Many people of faith in wealthy countries make regular donations to faith-related organizations such as World Jewish Relief, World Vision, Lutheran World Relief, and Catholic Relief Services to serve the poorest people in developing countries. This grant funding often spells the difference between survival and death for stricken people in times of emergency, as when earthquakes or storm-related disasters up-end peoples' lives. And they help to fund development projects such as irrigation works or health clinics that can make a world of difference for those living on the economic margins.

But like charitable donations in the United States, these efforts tap a relatively small capital base and help a relatively small population. Relief agencies typically cannot assist poor people who need capital to finance small-scale entrepreneurial initiatives, from making pottery or other crafts to the establishment of a neighborhood bakery. The creative energies and skills of these low-income people are largely untapped because their activities are considered to be too small and too risky to be underwritten by a commercial bank.

In the mid-1970s, a new concept in financing called microcredit was conceived to help those who have access neither to charitable giving nor to commercial loans. The idea is to make small loans available to start or support very small businesses, or microenterprises. Borrowers are typically poor people who lack the supplies, equipment, operating space, or other inputs needed to set up small shops or mini-factories, but who possess the skills and initiative needed to run a small business. A microcredit loan can help provide the needed inputs, and by nurturing a viable business, it can give people higher incomes and a better life. The concept was given a huge boost in the late 1990s when a group called the Microcredit Summit Campaign set a goal of serving some 100 million microborrowers by 2005, up from just 7 million in 1997. The Campaign was largely successful.[34]

Religious organizations have been part of this success. In fact, Oikocredit, which was founded by the World Council of Churches some three decades ago, is now the largest international private provider of microfinance services in the world.[35] It supplies more than $325 million annually to hundreds of microenterprises in 32 developing countries.[36] Some 60 percent of the credit it provides is microfinance.

Oikocredit is as unusual in the capital it raises as in the loans it makes. Investors are typically churches, religious communities, and religious individuals who can expect to earn 2 percent on their investment, usually well below the market rate. But Oikocredit investors are typically looking for a social return as much as a financial one, and are satisfied knowing that their full investment is making a much greater difference in the lives of the poor than their charitable donations could. Not only do investments typically involve larger sums than donations, they empower people in a way that grants often do not: borrowers get a loan for a project they believe in and can control, in contrast to grants, which may be subject to many conditions from lenders.

Despite its high profile in the world of microcredit, Oikocredit is arguably quite small compared to its potential. Most of the organization's capital comes from just 26,000 individuals or organizations in 20 countries, mostly wealthy. Yet in those countries, some 239 *million* Christians attend church regularly.[37] This means that for every churchgoing Christian in these countries who invests in Oikocredit, some 2,300 families do not, suggesting ample room for growth.[38]

The unfulfilled potential of Oikocredit is especially clear in the United States, where investments in Oikocredit total some $23 million, a tiny fraction of the estimated $6 trillion in total Christian-held investments in the country.[39] The bottom line: for every American Christian dollar invested in Oikocredit, about $261,000 is made in other investments.[40]

Oikocredit does not eliminate the need for direct grants to charities. Relief and development agencies do vital work and may lack a revenue stream that would allow them to qualify for a loan. Such agencies are still in need of grant aid. But Oikocredit does offer a powerful model for people seeking to leverage their wealth for greater good—and thereby strike a better balance between wealth and well-being in their lives and in the lives of their brothers and sisters around the world.

Investing Locally

A rapidly growing innovation in SRI is community investing, which provides capital to communities that are underserved by banks and other traditional financial institutions. The smallest area of SRI investment, community investing has nevertheless grown rapidly in the past decade, from $4.3 billion in 1995 to $17.5 billion in 2005 (in 2000 dollars), a fourfold increase.[41] And although it accounts for less than 1 percent of all SRI investments, community investing is nevertheless important because of the difference it can make in communities that desperately need financial capital.[42]

Proponents are excited about the growth in community investment and are working to expand its reach. The Social Investment Forum Foundation and Co-op America have launched a "1% or More in Community" campaign designed to encourage investors to switch some of their funds, whether banking or investments, into community banking. If successful, the campaign will boost the community-investing portfolio in the United States to more than $25 billion by 2007.[43]

One creative example of a community-investing institution is Charity Bank in the United Kingdom, which provides an innovative approach to saving and investing. Started in 2002, Charity Bank works like many other banks, taking deposits and making loans—but its loans go exclusively to charities or nonprofits. The bank uses investment from ethically minded savers and investors to grease the wheels of charitable work in the U.K. Charity Bank sees itself as a bank that allows people to "invest financial capital to build social capital."[44]

The bank's unique approach to finance helps fill a gap in community development. Its low overhead and charitable mission make it possible for the bank to make loans—typically for 5,000 to 500,000 British pounds ($9,300–$930,000)—that commercial banks would not consider. In the process, it increases access to capital for nonprofits that would otherwise be limited to the smaller pools of funds they can raise through donations. The arrangement combines the noble intentions of charity with the market discipline of a bank—hence the name.

A deposit at Charity Bank is like a supercharged charitable donation. Suppose a person makes a donation to charity of $20. That money helps the charity to do its work, but the benefit to the charity ends once the funds are spent. Suppose instead that the same person leverages his savings to drive his charitable giving. If he deposits $1,000 in a Charity Bank savings account, he can multiply his benefit to charity in two ways. First, he can accept less than the 2 percent interest the Bank normally pays, directing it to a charity of his choice, or donating it to Charity Bank. If he gives it to the bank, he essentially makes a gift of $20. The bank passes that gift along to its borrowers in the form of lower interest rates on loans. So the depositor reduces the cost that charitable operations must pay to borrow money.

But there's more: the $1,000 of savings is loaned to nonprofits to facilitate their work. As those nonprofits repay their loans, the capital is recycled and loaned to other nonprofits, again and again. All the while, the original savings of $1,000 belongs to the depositor, and can be reclaimed at any time.[45] In sum, the bank offers people a chance to direct some of their financial assets to sectors of society that need it badly, and that might otherwise have no access to capital. For this reason it promotes its operation as "banking for the common good."

As of the end of 2005, Charity Bank had authorized 480 loans worth 44 million British pounds ($82 million) to a broad range of nonprofits, from those engaged in social work, health, and community development to churches and organizations supporting the arts.[46] It is careful in making loans, and its clients have a good track record of loan repayments. Its pilot predecessor organization ran for six years without any losses. Charity Bank is proving that charities, churches, and community groups can be responsible borrowers, capable of generating their own income and developing strategic, independent thinking.

The potential for investment increases further if the government steps in to encourage this kind of saving, as the British government does in an effort to spur greater investment in depressed areas in the U.K. It offers tax breaks for citizens and corporations who invest funds in community investment banks. The benefit translates to a return on investment of 6–8 percent annually for five years, which is quite competitive with commercial savings.[47]

It is unreasonable, of course, to expect that all investments of religious people will be made at sub-par rates of return. But given the religious tradition of helping the poor, the huge amounts of capital that Americans own (and the larger amounts coming their way), and a new vision of progress that could reshape investment habits to include the well-being of the poor, it arguably *is* reasonable to suppose that all investments by religious people be ethical. Some might go into screened investments that earn competitive rates of interest, and some might be steered to investments that help the poor and offer a modest yield. Religious people in wealthy countries are in an enviable position: they often have enough wealth, and, increasingly, the creative institutions, to move their societies closer to the ideals to which they are committed.

PART FOUR

Inspiring Progress

CHAPTER 10

New Vison:
Toward an Ethics of Progress

"We have committed the Golden Rule to memory;
let us now commit it to life."
—Edwin Markham[1]

D eveloping an ethic of bounded creativity is not easy in a
world accustomed to open-ended technological and economic development. Indeed, many sages of our time have
warned that humans lack the ethical muscles needed to work through
the great challenges of this era. In her 1963 classic, *Silent Spring*, Rachel
Carson asserted that humans live in "the Neanderthal age of biology
and philosophy," particularly in our assumption that nature is merely
a tool for human use.[2] Physicist and cosmologist Brian Swimme has
observed that humans are now a "macrophase" presence on the
planet, with an impact comparable to glaciation, erosion, or other
geological forces, but that we possess a "microphase" capacity for judg-
ment.[3] And Thomas Berry has written that while human ethical traditions can deal with suicide, genocide, and homicide, they have little
to say about "biocide" (the degradation and loss of the life systems
of the Earth) and "geocide" (the devastation of the Earth itself).[4]

These are sobering assessments, but they need not be the last word.
Humans can be as creative and responsive to the moral challenges
of the 21st century as we were to the scientific and technological puz-
zles of the last. Indeed, Berry himself notes that the world's religions
and philosophical traditions can help, in part because of their understanding of the importance of limits. The Hindu concept of *dharma*

(right conduct), the *dao* (underlying law of the universe) of Daoism and *li* (social propriety) of Confucianism, and the Greek concepts of *dike* (the order of justice) and *logos* (the ordering principle of the universe) all suggest in the broadest sense that human development happens within limits.[5] The traditional religious interest in limits suggests that religions could be useful partners in rebuilding the eroded banks—of ecological integrity and human well-being—of the river of progress in the 21st century.

Reclaiming Community

Working out the specifics of an ethics of bounded creativity will likely take decades, but finding a better balance between the individual and the collective will surely figure prominently in the discussion. Confucian scholar Tu Weiming has argued that a major problem with the Enlightenment approach to progress is its "conspicuous absence of the idea of community."[6]

Few would argue that the Enlightenment worldview, with the many powerful political, social, and scientific advances it has given the world, needs to be scrapped entirely. A more reasonable prescription is to expand Enlightenment values to include stronger social and ecological dimensions. "We need to explore the spiritual resources that may help us to broaden the scope of the Enlightenment project (and) deepen its moral sensitivity so that it can realize its full potential as a worldview for the entire human community," Tu writes.[7] Part of this process, he notes, will be to complement the Enlightenment emphasis on the individual and individual interest with a fuller view of individual well-being. This fuller view roots the individual in community and is summarized in the ethic, "in order to establish myself, I have to help others to establish themselves."[8] In contrast to the rugged individualist perspective that assumes—and expects—that each of us will make our own way in the world largely independently, Professor Tu offers a perspective of fundamental interdependence. Our lives are interconnected, and the well-being of each of us has a social as well as an individual dimension.

Fortunately, the world's faith traditions have a great deal to offer to the effort to reclaim community. From the West, notes Dr. Tu, the

Greek understanding of citizenship, Judaism's notion of covenant, and Christianity's emphasis on universal love all have contributions to make in bolstering the values of community. From the East, Hinduism, Jainism, Buddhism, Confucianism, and Daoism, along with Islam, offer an understanding of more cooperative, community oriented, and less self-interested societies. And indigenous traditions have a rich tradition of geographic rootedness and values of mutuality, reciprocity, and intimate relationship with nature that could be invaluable in strengthening modern communities.[9] A new understanding of progress this century would profit greatly from religious wisdom underscoring the value of strong communities.

The effort to reclaim community should include broadening our understanding of community to include the natural world on which humans radically depend. It will require an "anthropocosmic" worldview—an understanding of humans as embedded in the cosmic order—in place of the Enlightenment view of humans as being apart from nature.[10] It will be deeply relational, with a web as the appropriate metaphor, so that humans understand profoundly their intimate connection to all of creation. An anthropocosmic worldview would affect the way we think about everything, from law to education to the way we build our economies.

The details of an ethics that reclaims community and that embraces the natural world will be an evolving effort. But based on the problems created by our current worldview, and on the reflections of ecologists, sociologists, economists, theologians, and others interested in building sustainable societies, we can identify some of the questions that will likely need to be answered if we are to create a new and sustainable understanding of progress over the coming century.[11] (See Table 10–1, pp. 148–149.)

Global Norms?

The values-laden questions in Table 10–1 are discussed largely among specialists interested in sustainable development. But in at least two cases in the past decade, religions have been involved in efforts to establish a set of global values in line with the ones suggested in the table.

TABLE 10–1. Questions to Shape a New Ethics for the 21st Century

Dimension	Questions
Role of Human Beings	Can we reshape our place in the world, so that human ingenuity flourishes within ecological boundaries?
Nature and Natural Resources	Can we appreciate not just the economic value of nature, but also its ecological, aesthetic, and even spiritual value?
	Can we reclaim a sense of wonder vis-à-vis nature?
	To what extent should the great resources of the Earth—the air, sea, and land—be regarded as commons?
	Can we appreciate the complexity of nature and interact with it in a humble and sensitive way?
Land	Can we re-establish a rootedness and appreciation of place?
	Can we see ourselves less as owners of real estate and more as inhabitants of a bioregion?
Property	Should ownership of property carry obligations to the environment and to the community?
Law	Should laws protect only the rights of humans, or does nature have rights as well—for example, the right of a species not to be driven to extinction?
Education	Can we ensure that university graduates are not merely empowered despoilers of the environment, but are trained in wisdom—to understand nature, human communities, and how the two best relate to each other?
	Can we develop interdisciplinary training so that students understand webs of relationships?

TABLE 10—1 CONTINUED

Science	Can we root scientific research in a paradigm of whole systems?
	Can we ensure that science is carried out in the public interest, rather than at the behest of the highest bidder?
Industry	Can the regenerative and zero-waste properties of natural processes become the model for our industries?
Technology	Can we rely primarily on renewable energy and on appropriately sized technologies?
	Can we design our infrastructure, products, and services so that the use of virgin materials is kept to a minimum?
Economics	Can we root our economies within healthy ecologies?
	Should strengthening local economies be a priority?
	Can we acknowledge that sustainable economies will need to limit growth in virgin resource use?
	Can we consume in a way that is consistent with personal and community well-being?
Agriculture	Can we make our agriculture regenerative?
	Can we design farms that make minimal or zero use of pesticides and chemical fertilizers, while delivering bountiful, nutritious food to all people?
Social Values	Can we learn to respect and value differences, commit to the inherent dignity of all human beings, and reject extreme inequality?
	Should we regard basic needs such as food, water, shelter, and health care as basic rights?
Politics	Should we move toward greater political decentralization, greater grassroots empowerment, and a strong commitment to nonviolence?

Source: See Endnote 11 for Chapter 10.

The first was the Earth Charter, a set of principles for the global community that seeks "to establish a sound ethical foundation for the emerging global society and to help build a sustainable world." [12] It promotes a respect for nature, diversity, universal human rights, economic justice, and a culture of peace. Unlike past efforts to articulate a global consensus on important values, such as the Universal Declaration of Human Rights, the Earth Charter is primarily an effort of civil society, rather than governments. The draft Charter was developed in a three-year long consultation with citizens and organizations from the civil sector, including religious groups. [13] The Charter is also unusual in the unprecedented importance it gives to environmental well-being as a prerequisite for human advancement. Indeed, the Charter starts with the Earth and moves to the human, in recognition of our planet as the platform on which all human activities are built.

Since its completion in 2000, the Earth Charter has been discussed by citizens' groups around the world in an effort to raise awareness of the effort. Some religious communities, for example, have been active in using the document in schools and as a guide for planning future ministry work. On the political front, promoters of the document sought recognition for it at the World Summit on Sustainable Development in Johannesburg, South Africa, in 2002, and succeeded in securing the endorsement of several heads of state, although references to the Earth Charter were not included in the final version of the political declaration that emerged from the Summit. How successful the Earth Charter will be in developing a worldwide consensus on fundamental ethics remains to be seen, but promoters are reorganizing in 2006 to launch a new effort to give the Charter greater traction.

The second major effort to suggest a set of global values emerged directly from the global religious community in the 1990s. The Global Ethic, a project spearheaded by Swiss theologian Hans Küng, was a research initiative meant to identify common ethical tenets of the world's religions, as a way of defining a globally relevant ethical foundation appropriate in an age of globalization. Collaborating with scholars from religious traditions around the world, Küng found that virtually all religions place great value on two principles: The first is that all human beings, no matter their station in life, possess an inherent dignity and must be treated humanely. The second is what is often dubbed "The Golden Rule," i.e., Do unto others as you would have them do unto you. Because of the universal appeal of these precepts, Küng has labeled it the Global Ethic. His research also found general agreement on subprinciples that mandate that people not kill, steal, lie, or abuse based on gender.

The Global Ethic is not meant to replace the ethical teachings of the world's religions, but instead to highlight the common base of ethical belief of the vast majority of the world's people. Indeed, its fresh articulation of ancient wisdoms could help create a new global ethical consciousness for several reasons. First, the Ethic has a broad base of support: Küng's research was endorsed as the principal conference outcome of the 1993 Parliament of the World's Religions, a historic gathering of thousands of religious leaders and lay people from the world's religious and spiritual traditions. This support helped raise worldwide awareness that this ancient ethical wisdom is shared broadly across cultures and across time, and therefore is a potentially powerful common ground for societal and international relations in this young century.

In addition, the Global Ethic is given respectful nods, if not outright endorsement, by some political leaders. United Nations Secretary-General Kofi Annan convened a group of "eminent persons" in 2001, the International Year of Dialogue Among Civilizations, to study the potential for a new paradigm for international relations in an age of globalization. The group, which included, in addition to Küng, Nobel Prize-winning economist Amartya Sen, former European Commission president Jacques Delor, former German president Richard von Weisäcker, Professor Tu Weiming, Nobel Prize-winning novelist Nadine Gordimer, and Prince Hassan of Jordan, eventually published a report, "Crossing the Divide: Dialogue Among Civilizations." [14] The report embraces the need for a common ethical foundation for global relations, in language that is similar to that of the Global Ethic.

British Prime Minister Tony Blair, former president of Ireland and U.N. High Commissioner for Human Rights Mary Robinson, President of Germany Horst Köhler, and 2003 Nobel Peace Prize winner Shirin Ebadi have all traveled to Küng's research center at Tübingen University to give Global Ethic lectures. Prime Minister Blair noted in 2000 that, "the inevitability of globalisation demands a parallel globalisation of our best ethical values."[15] Secretary-General Annan made similar statements in 2003, and noted in his address that ethics cannot be dismissed for being visionary. "Ought implies can," he said, meaning that if a set of values like those in the Global Ethic are morally desirable, they are also doable.[16]

Ethics in Action

The Global Ethic could also have widespread impact because its ancient precepts are meant to be applied to the great issues of our day, and not just to interpersonal relations. As public awareness of the global sustainability crisis grows, and given the relatively broad base of collaboration in developing the Earth Charter and the Global Ethic, it is plausible to imagine that these initiatives could begin to influence the human community's approach to global problems.

Consider, for example, how climate change might look from the perspective of the Global Ethic. At the heart of the climate issue is a fundamental injustice: some of the countries most responsible for creating the problem are the least committed to solving it—hardly a model of the "do unto others" standard set out by the Global Ethic. Applying the Global Ethic to climate change would highlight this injustice in terms meaningful to a broad swath of humanity. And solutions to the challenge that treat countries according to the values of the Global Ethic might receive a needed boost.

The so-called "Contraction and Convergence" (C&C) initiative of the Global Commons Institute in the United Kingdom, for example, might be attractive from the perspective of the Global Ethic. C&C seeks to reduce carbon emissions in industrial countries (contraction) while distributing future credits for carbon emissions on an equalized per person basis globally (convergence).[17] Its core principle is equity: the right to pollute should be capped, then spread equally across the human family—essentially treating everyone the way each of us might want to be treated if our place on the planet were randomly assigned. In addition, because the C&C plan would tax nations that exceed their emissions quotas and use the proceeds to help meet the Millennium Development Goals and other vital development objectives, the C&C would support the second principle of the Global Ethic, that all people are endowed with inherent dignity.

The initiative has gained the support of religious leaders, including a powerful statement by the Archbishop of Canterbury, leader of the world's Anglicans and Episcopalians, in July 2004. The C&C initiative, he said, "appears utopian only if we refuse to contemplate the alternatives honestly."[18] But imagine if religious leaders globally were to articulate a link between the Global Ethic and climate change. Then the Archbishop might be joined by the leaders of a wide range of religious traditions, all speaking from a common and broadly understood ethical foundation. The pressure on political leaders to seek a more equitable solution to the climate challenge could be intense.

Action as Ethics

Lest winning full global support for efforts like the Earth Charter or the Global Ethic seem too slow in a world gripped by a growing set of crises, the good news is that a global ethical framework need not be finalized before action can happen. Indeed, ethics is not purely a philosophical exercise, but emerges from and is formed by the realities of daily life. One of the precepts of the "liberation theology" movement that emerged in Latin America in the 1970s and 80s, for example, is the notion that theology today best proceeds from people's "lived experience," rather than from abstract principles.[19] "The act of engagement will itself spur new thinking, new understanding," writes environmental writer Bill McKibben, who is also active in his local church.[20] He cites U.S. civil rights activist Rosa Parks' refusal to surrender her seat on a bus in 1955 as an act that led to new appreciation for the power of the Jewish story of the Exodus, with its theme of liberation.[21] In that case, action came first and reflection followed, and the result was a deeper appreciation for the living nature of sacred writings.

E. F. Schumacher picks up the theme, using explicitly Christian language. "Ideas can change the world only by some process of 'incarnation,'" he says.[23] Ethics must be grounded in action, and further, this action should be rooted in the imagined future rather than in the status quo. The Interfaith Power and Lights of the world, or the environmentalist Buddhist monks or the Charity Banks, have committed themselves to actions rooted in a worldview that has not fully arrived. They are examples of the famous exhortation of Mahatma Gandhi that we need to "be the change you want to see in the world."[23]

CHAPTER 11

Getting to a New Progress

*"It is the vocation of the prophet to keep alive the ministry
of the imagination, to keep on conjuring and proposing
futures alternative to the single one the king wants to urge
as the only thinkable one."*
—Walter Brueggeman[1]

Creating a new understanding of progress is an ambitious,
even audacious, task. But it is an unavoidable responsibility—
"the great work" of our generation, to borrow from the title
of Thomas Berry's most recent book. Changing our fundamental
relationship to nature and redefining the purpose of our economies
and obligations to other human beings is a far greater challenge than
sending a man to the moon, cracking the human genome, or any other
technological challenge ever undertaken, because it is more sweep-
ing and because it involves changing the way people view the world
and their place in it. It requires transforming what E. F. Schumacher
has called "the people of the forward stampede" (those of us who are
socialized to embrace the more, more, more version of progress) into
"homecomers," people who re-value place, relationships, and other
simple but profound pleasures in life.[2]

All sectors of society—government, business, the media, universities, nongovernmental organizations (NGOs), and all elements of civil
society—will need to be engaged in this task. But because the shift is
fundamentally about a change in values (from which appropriate technologies and policies will flow), the world's wisdom traditions will be

especially important partners. The world's religions understand and speak the values vernacular, and they help us define our place in the world. It is difficult to imagine success in building a new understanding of progress without their active engagement. Religions are the heavy hitters needed for such a massive societal transformation.

Rebuilding the ecological and well-being banks of the river of progress will take time and will likely vary from culture to culture. But it will surely deal with three main areas of activity: appreciating nature, building strong communities, and rethinking the way we consume.

Appreciating Nature

To say that people in industrial countries are environmentally illiterate is to choose the wrong metaphor. The problem is not only that we lack the science; we are handicapped by a lack of intimacy with nature. Better to think of ourselves as environmentally orphaned, a people with little direct knowledge of the natural world that sustains us. Many of us, for example, may be hard pressed to name the three most common flowers, trees, and birds in our town. Or how much rainfall we get annually. Or what will happen to our region under scenarios of climate change. Because our contact with nature is often indirect—many of us spend a good part of our day indoors on computers and telephones, and get our food and other vital purchases out-of-package from retail outlets—it's easy to see how our lives are increasingly disconnected from the natural world.

A new progress will require that we be reintroduced to nature. "We will not fight to save what we do not love," wrote Harvard biologist Stephen Jay Gould in his argument that people form "an emotional and spiritual bond" between themselves and nature.[3] By helping believers appreciate the sacred dimension of nature, religions can teach us to love the environment around us. Faith-sponsored education on the environment (or Creation, or whatever term works best in each tradition) can help to build this affective connection to nature.

Some of this education can happen indoors, but religious institutions often have wonderful opportunities to ground it meaningfully in the natural environment itself. The Living Churchyards initiative in the U.K., which uses church property to allow the wild to flourish, is a good example of a field opportunity for a spiritual appreciation of nature. But many other examples exist as well. Since 1997, the Alliance of Religions and Conservation (ARC) has sponsored a Sacred Land project, which promotes the use of gardens, wells, pilgrimage routes, trees, art and other religious assets to connect with the natural world. Walkers have established a path in Wales, for example, that connects 16 Cistercian monasteries, and which will become the longest footpath in Wales when it officially opens in 2008.[4] The Jamyang Buddhist Center in South London is planning to convert the parking lot of an abandoned property into a sacred garden.[5] And villagers in North Cornwall restored a "holy well" that dates at least to the 15th century as part of a Sacred Land grant.[6] Projects like those are wonderful ways not only to preserve the natural world, but to help congregants understand what that world is. Indeed, a year's worth of Earth Sundays and eco-kashrut practices will be of little use if we have no intimate understanding of what we are celebrating.

At the same time, it is helpful in many traditions to ensure that people are part of nature education as well. For traditions accustomed to dealing with issues of justice, but less accustomed to thinking of the sacred dimension of nature, it is perhaps helpful to make the human connection on environmental issues. Thus, the efforts of schools like Colegio Santa Maria in São Paulo to reach out to slum dwellers as part of its environmental education packs an inspirational double punch for students, teaching them to love neighbor and nature in a single effort.

Religious rituals and celebrations involve education of a different sort, a conversion of the heart and spirit. As such, they are another opportunity for congregants to learn to love the natural world. We have seen that Buddhist monks have "ordained" trees, and some Jews are interested in extending the ethical underpinnings of kashrut to include environmental values as ways of adapting tradition to modern circumstances. Episcopalians have for more than two decades celebrated the "Earth Mass" at New York's Cathedral Church of St. John the Divine on the feast of St. Francis of Assisi, which features a procession of animals down the aisle.[7] And Earth Sunday in April and Creation Sunday in September are now regular features of some

Christian liturgical calendars. All of these initiatives adapt existing rituals to embrace an environmental dimension.

Some congregations may be uncomfortable with such adaptations. They might instead consider ways to use standard rituals to highlight the value of a healthy environment. Many religions, for example, use water in ritual washings before prayers. It goes without saying that use of polluted water for this purpose would be sacrilegious: is it equally unacceptable to tolerate polluted rivers, lakes, and streams *outside* of worship? Or consider food rituals, such as the blessing before meals, or the Hindu tradition of *prasad*, the sacred ritual offerings of food.[8] Could these rituals be used to highlight the importance of food that is grown and delivered in a sustainable way?

Creating Well-Being

Through their spiritual work and social services, religions strengthen the well-being of their members and the communities they live in. By running soup kitchens, clinics, orphanages, job assistance programs, and other social services, for example, they help to cover the basic needs—the bedrock of well-being—of society's poorest. They also support and encourage the more transcendent values at the high end of the well-being spectrum, like spiritual growth and freedom. Perhaps less appreciated are the contributions that congregations make to relationship building, a critically important value of well-being. Through their capacity to build strong internal communities, and through their connections to the larger communities in which they are rooted, congregations are important builders and sustainers of nurturing relationships. Guided by a new vision of progress, this community-building service could be more critical than ever.

In a world of growing oil scarcity and concerns about globalization, people may find increasing value in strengthening local economies. Congregations can help support local merchants through their institutional purchases and by influencing the purchases of individual congregants. The initiatives of the Interfaith Climate and Energy Initiative in Maine to support local farmers is a good example of this. Individual commitments to buying at least $10 of food purchases per week from local suppliers, and seasonal subscriptions with local farmers to purchase their produce, help ensure that farmers get local business and a higher share of each consumer's food dollar. Moreover, to the extent that community-supported agriculture (CSA) subscriptions are a congregational rather than individual initiative, CSAs can be a bonding experience for the church community. Myriad other ways to strengthen local economies are available to congregations, from local purchases of supplies, to support for a "living wage," to encouraging business initiatives that add value to local exports. By strengthening the ability of local communities to provide for themselves, congregations can help build resilient economies of well-being.

Religious groups can also be watchful for opportunities to strengthen families, the nucleus of all communities. Congregations and religious organizations can encourage government and business policies that offer leave for new parents, adequate annual vacation, and affordable daycare for working families. Initiatives like these can help families reclaim time, an increasingly scarce resource that is vital for strengthening and maintaining relationships.

Indeed, religious groups might consider weighing in on re-structuring the basic societal bargain of the 20th century, under which increases in business productivity are rewarded with higher wages, rather than the alternative: increased leisure time. The bargain of the last century raised living standards and gave people access to a cornucopia of goods. But it also led to increased environmental problems, higher levels of indebtedness, and for some, longer working hours to make ends meet. In societies that have already reached a high level of material prosperity, it may be time to open a dialogue about whether workers might be better served with more time off rather than higher wages as the reward for increased productivity. The benefits could be manifold: more time with family and friends, and lessened environmental impact that would accompany more moderate levels of spending.

Rethinking our Material Lives

The great historian Arnold Toynbee once noted that the measure of a civilization's growth is not its capacity to build empires or raise living standards, but the Law of Progressive Simplification: the capacity to spend more and more time and energy on the nonmaterial side of life.[10] In an age of rampant consumerism, this call to greatness may sound out of touch—but to people of faith, perhaps also comforting and familiar, given the importance of spirituality in religious traditions everywhere. The world's religions have the capacity to challenge their institutions and adherents to make Toynbee's vision a reality.

The place to start is to review existing consumption with an eye to making it efficient and ethical. Through their teaching and through their own purchases, congregations can highlight opportunities to purchase fair trade or organically produced goods; green energy; materials with a high level of recycled content; more efficient cars, appliances, and heating systems; and goods made by workers who receive a just wage. It is easy to forget that consumers hold real power to send a message of ethics and justice via the market, but houses of worship are in a strong position to remind us regularly to use this power well.

But consuming ethically is not the same as consuming less. Religious groups are also well positioned to help adherents reflect on their lifestyle and consider whether they would be better off simplifying their lives. Many people in industrial countries are overworked and indebted and lack time for family and friends. Many also complain that they have little time for spiritual reading, prayer, reflective walks, or other quiet activities that strengthen spiritual development. Living more simply could bring relief for all of these problems and considerably enhance personal well-being. And as people become more skilled at "downshifting," or living more simply, they are likely to have more time or money to offer to their community. In sum, simplifying can help us to shape lives of greater well-being, strengthen our communities, and improve the well-being of those less fortunate as well.

At some level, we know these arguments to be true, even attractive, but they are seldom compelling enough to persuade us to change our lifestyles. Consumerism has the grip of an addiction, and we need help to break it. It is ironic that houses of worship in the United States have been leaders for decades in offering 12-step programs in their basements as an outreach service to people fighting drug or alcohol addiction. It may be time to offer a similar sustainability-related service to one's own congregation. The "simplicity circle" approach of the online Simple Living Network, while not a 12-step program, offers a creative mechanism for people to explore simplicity in a supportive and encouraging setting.[10] The circles could easily be adapted for use in congregations, and with the support of congregation leaders could be just the tool that moves congregants from thinking about simplicity to acting on it.

Congregations and religious organizations might also help people come to terms with the moral dimension of wealth, especially in prosperous countries where religious people are in a position to use their wealth to create a better world. This can happen through workshops and retreats like the ones offered by the aptly named Ministry of Money in Germantown, Maryland. Its retreats on Money and Faith, Kids and Money, and similar topics, along with pilgrimages to poor nations that bring congregants face to face with the realities of poverty, challenge prosperous people to think differently about their wealth in a non-judgmental and supportive setting.[11]

Religious groups could also ensure that congregations are aware of opportunities to leverage their wealth for good, through investment options that steer financing to those unserved by commercial banks. And clear goals for religious wealth could be discussed and set. Imagine, for example, if the concept of tithing were adapted for use with investments, so that 10 percent of a person's investments were directed to community development banks, microfinance organizations, and other entities that offer financing to organizations that help the poor. Redirecting wealth in this way could greatly increase the capital available to poor people for whom a lack of financing is the greatest obstacle to a better life. And it would give investors the satisfaction of knowing that their wealth is being leveraged for good far beyond their charitable giving.

Finally, religious groups can help critique the advertising and media influences that drive so many of our material cravings. Some are already active in this area: in one of his earliest statements as the Archbishop of Canterbury, Rowan Williams expressed strong concern about the media and its impact on children, and a few churches and synagogues are promoting TV Turnoff Week as a way to encourage congregants to shun the content of modern media and to strengthen ties with families and friends through non-media activities. But the faith community could have a much stronger impact if more leaders and organizations protested violence and sexual exploitation in television programming. A collective religious effort to set standards for advertising on children's programming, for example, could be a start in loosening the grip of consumerism on our culture.

Leveraging Religious Influence

Beyond the specific activities that can create a new understanding of progress, the way religions go about this work can be important. By tapping religious assets, stressing the positive, collaborating when possible, and returning to the power of one's own tradition, it is possible to make major progress in educating about nature, building communities, and rethinking consumption.

Tap Religious Assets

Individual congregations are often one node in a huge network of religious bodies that might include regional, national, and international governing organizations; hospitals, schools, orphanages, and other social service groups; print, radio, and television offices; missionary, relief, and development organizations; and religiously-affiliated NGOs, to name just a few. And the network gets much larger when the web of one denomination or religion begins to make connections to the webs of others. Such networks have huge potential to leverage change, but they are likely underused, even from the perspective of a single religion or denomination.

Just as hierarchical religions use their centralized religious structures to set the teachings for an entire diocese, nation, or even the world, these structures can also be useful in disseminating sustainability policy across a wide area. The Diocese of Manchester in the U.K. does this with its environmental policy, issued in November 2003, which guides the operations of diocesan churches and is meant to be a model for individual lifestyles as well. The policy calls for efficient use of energy and water, adoption of renewable energy, commitment to recycling and materials reuse, reliance on electronic rather than paper communications where possible, and minimizing travel, especially by automobile.[12]

Religious webs can also be used to advance ethical consumption, while saving money. Martin Palmer of ARC notes, for example, that the Anglican Church in the U.K. could use its "faith structure"—its network of assets—to green its churches and negotiate better purchasing contracts. With an estimated 38,000 buildings, the Church of England can approach green energy companies, sellers of recycled paper and fair trade coffee, and other ethically-oriented suppliers and ask for a package deal in return for the church's massive business. Overworked parish staffs have neither the time nor the clout to do such bulk purchasing on their own. And to the degree that ethical goods are more expensive—often the case with organic produce, green electricity, and other such goods—individual cash-strapped congregations could benefit from group purchasing that makes those goods more affordable. The more extended the network, of course, the better the deal that could be struck. In many countries, a religious purchasing network could be the single largest purchaser in some markets, after governments.

Sometimes the extended religious network is larger than people commonly realize. Reverend Jim Ball of the Evangelical Environmental Network notes that as EEN considers its work on climate change in the coming years, it is working with Christian relief and development organizations to ensure that they understand the issue and its implications for their work. "[For] any development project that's going to last more than five years, they need to factor in climate change. They need to plan for this, to adapt," Ball says. And because the relief agencies will be affected, he says, they have a direct interest in becoming involved in the policy and advocacy work. "We can try to get them involved in meetings on [Capitol] Hill, and get them to talk to their constituencies about this."[13]

Stress the Positive

The idea that restraint and limits are key to a sustainable future is a tough message to market, but it can be framed more positively. The most important part of restraint is that it can facilitate greater creativity and well-being in the long run, just as good eating does. Diets are not marketed by emphasizing what a person cannot eat, but on the promise of greater energy, happiness, and self-esteem. In the same way, promotion of an ethic of bounded creativity should focus on the positive endgame of a new progress. Religions understand this, suggests ARC's Palmer, which is why seasons of sacrifice such as Lent, Ramadan, or Yom Kippur are not ends in themselves, but culminate in celebration.[14]

Environmental writer Bill McKibben, who is active in his local church, tells the story of the difficulty of getting fellow church members to embrace the "$100 Christmas" program, which urged congregants to limit their holiday expenditures to $100. "When we began we were long-faced, talking about the environmental damage that Christmas caused (all those batteries!), the money that could instead go to social justice work, and so on. But we found that this did not do the trick, either for us of for our fellow congregants. What did the trick, we discovered, was focusing on happier holidays.... We talked about making Christmas more fun."[15] By emphasizing families, friends, and fun, McKibben writes, people experienced a deeply joyful Christmas in spite of—or perhaps in part because of—the $100 limit.

Fun is contagious, and showing people they could have more fun in a sustainable world may be a key to spreading the message of a new progress. As McKibben notes, "The only way to make people doubt, even for a minute, the inevitability of their course in life is to show them that they are being cheated of the truest happiness."[16] This is why the Center for a New American Dream, a U.S. organization that promotes a higher quality of life, uses the slogan "More fun, less stuff" in its work.[17]

Collaborate Whenever Possible

The environmental and social issues involved in redefining progress are huge, and collaboration among religions and denominations is likely to increase the possibilities for successful engagement of them. Models of successful collaboration—especially across religions, not just within denominations—can maximize the effectiveness of religious partnerships. Organizations such as the National Religious Partnership on the Environment (NRPE), the European Christian Environmental Network, the World Council of Churches, and others stand as useful examples of how religions and denominations might work well together.

Another model for interreligious collaboration is the World Conference of Religions for Peace (WCRP), a New York-based group that promotes religious cooperation on conflict resolution, human rights, child and family issues, peace education, disarmament, and development and environment.[18] Operating in 55 countries, WCRP uses a mechanism called Interreligious Councils (IRCs), composed of respected religious leaders of various faiths, to address tough issues in each nation. The IRCs bring together recognized and respected leaders of different groups who can speak credibly for their religion or denomination. By building trust among the leaders, these issue-driven interfaith groups are able to "bring the power of the collective voice to bear on pressing issues," according to WCRP Director of the Program on Children Jim Cairns. IRCs are "a durable mechanism for cooperation" that can be used to address issue after issue over time, he adds.

The IRCs have had some notable successes. Muslim and Christian leaders, for example, have worked to mediate two civil wars in Liberia, and to combat HIV/AIDS in Uganda. IRCs have also mediated among warring factions in Sierra Leone and helped ease ethnic tensions in Bosnia and Kosovo.[19] The potential of this kind of collaboration for building sustainable societies is clear. Imagine religious leaders getting together regularly to voice their support for renewable energy, opposition to oil drilling, or recommendation of adequate health care for all. Bringing together the moral power of religions to speak with one voice could be a powerful way for religious communities to help shape a new vision of progress.

Retreat to Your Own Corner

As vital as collaboration is, the most important source of religious power is found in a tradition's own origins: in the charisma of its founder, the wisdom of its scriptures, and the stories that speak deeply to believers. A religion's most authentic response to today's global crises is likely to emerge from its core inspiration. This is why interfaith organizations like ARC and NRPE do not create one-size-fits-all programs for their diverse members, but allow each to participate to the extent and in the way that is most authentic.

But religious people need to have confidence in the power and truth of their own sacred texts. Only to the extent that religious people take seriously their teachings—about the inherent dignity of all people, the need to treat others as we would be treated, and, increasingly, the need to care for the natural environment—will the power of those teachings be unleashed. Benedictine Sister Joan Chittister framed the issue well in an address to a conference of the Network of Spiritual Progressives in May 2006: "Do we need the culture to be religious?" she asked. "No, my friends, we need religions to be religious."[20] Treated seriously, religious scrolls can release what theologian Daniel Maguire of the University of Notre Dame has called "theopolitical dynamite—a dynamic and powerful vision of what life can be," and in the process, help change whole societies for the better.[21]

Unleashing this power, however, requires religious people to bring their values to the public square. Too often, especially in industrialized countries, values questions are treated as private matters that have no place in public discourse. But to leave one's values at home is to assent to the status quo of excessive individualism, consumerism, commodification of myriad aspects of life, environmental decline, and the absence of strong communities. The religious community's gift—to articulate the ethical and spiritual dimensions of modern issues—is indispensable to full public discussion of the pressing challenges of our day, and to developing a new understanding of human progress in the 21st century.

Appendix

Organizations Working on Sustainable Development Issues

INTERFAITH COLLABORATION

Alliance of Religions and Conservation
A nongovernmental organization that helps the major religions of the world develop their own environmental programs.
www.arcworld.org

Council for a Parliament of the World's Religions
A group that promotes harmony among the world's religions and seeks to engage them on major global issues through various fora and events.
www.cpwr.org

Forum on Religion and Ecology
A resource-rich website with writings and activities related to sustainability from major world religions.
www.environment.harvard.edu/religion/religion

Global Ethic Foundation
An organization that promotes use of the Global Ethic worldwide.
www.global-ethic.org

GreenFaith
An interfaith organization that promotes green building, religious environmental education, and environmental advocacy.
www.greenfaith.org

National Religious Partnership on the Environment
A partnership of the Coalition on the Environment and Jewish Life, Evangelical Environmental Network, National Council of Churches, and U.S. Conference of Catholic Bishops to promote care of the environment.
www.nrpe.org

Network of Spiritual Progressives
An organization dedicated to bringing progressive religious values into U.S. politics.
www.spiritualprogressives.org

Religion, Science, and the Environment
An organization that spreads scientific and spiritual awareness of the human threat to the natural world, especially waters. Sponsors the Ecumenical Patriarchate's shipboard symposia.
www.rsesymposia.org

United Religions Initiative
A network community that promotes interfaith cooperation and seeks to end religiously motivated violence.
www.uri.org

Web of Creation
An interfaith organization providing online environmental resources for faith-based communities.
www.webofcreation.org

ACTIVITIES SPECIFIC TO PARTICULAR DENOMINATIONS OR RELIGIONS

A Rocha: Christians in Conservation
A Christian network of activists and scientists engaged in environmental conservation in Europe and the United States.
www.arocha.org

The Bahá'ís: Social and Economic Development
The international website of the Bahá'í faith, with resources on social and economic development issues.
http://bahai.org/dir/social_action/sed

Catholic Conservation Center
An online-only group that aims to promote ecology, environmental justice, and stewardship in light of the traditions of the Catholic Church.
http://conservation.catholic.org

Coalition on the Environment and Jewish Life
A coalition of Jewish organizations devoted to care of the environment.
www.coejl.org

Earth Ministry
A Christian ecumenical organization that works to build a just and
sustainable world.
www.earthministry.org

Eco-Justice Ministries
An ecumenical agency that helps churches develop social justice and
environmental sustainability ministries.
www.eco-justice.org

Evangelical Environmental Network
A network of evangelical Christians concerned about Creation Care
(environmental issues).
www.creationcare.org

Islamic Foundation for Ecology and Environmental Sciences
An organization that articulates the Islamic position on environmental
matters and attempts to give practical manifestation to this.
www.ifees.org

Islam Science, Environment, and Technology
A clearinghouse for Islamic perspectives on science and the environment.
www.islamset.com/env/index.html

Khalsa Environment Project
A Sikh initiative that seeks to build a more environmentally robust
world.
www.khalsaenvironmentproject.org

National Council of Churches, Eco-Justice Programs
A site detailing the environmental initiatives of the NCC, the umbrella
organization of Protestant Christian Churches in the United States.
www.nccecojustice.org

The Noah Project:
Jewish Education, Celebration, and Action of the Earth
An organization that raise environmental awareness within the Jewish
community through education, celebration of festivals, and practical
action.
www.noahproject.org.uk

Soka-Gakkai International
A Buddhist organization that promotes peace, culture, and education.
www.sgi.org

Target Earth
A U.S. Christian group active in 15 countries that works in the service of the Earth and the poor.
www.targetearth.org

U.S. Conference of Catholic Bishops, Environmental Justice Program
A site with useful environmental resources and activities for Catholic dioceses and parishes.
www.usccb.org/sdwp/ejp/index.html

World Council of Churches: Justice, Peace, and Creation
The environmental site of the WCC, representing more than 340 Christian churches, denominations, and church fellowships in over 100 countries and territories.
wcc-coe.org/wcc/what/jpc/index-e.html

SOCIALLY RESPONSIBLE INVESTMENT

Charity Bank
An organization that lends to charities and provides a way for investors to have their wealth be managed for the benefit of communities.
www.charitybank.org

International Interfaith Investment Group (3iG)
An organization that promotes responsible investment by religious bodies worldwide.
www.3ignet.org

Interfaith Center on Corporate Responsibility
An association of faith-based institutions that seek to invest their wealth responsibly.
www.iccr.org

Oikocredit
An ethical investment fund that finances projects in developing countries.
www.oikocredit.org

Social Investment Forum
A U.S. nonprofit organization that promotes the concept, practice, and growth of socially responsible investing.
www.socialinvest.org

CONSUMERISM AND SIMPLE LIVING

Overcoming Consumerism
A site with resources for simplifying one's life.
www.verdant.net

Alternatives for Simple Living
A Christian organization dedicated to simpler living.
www.simpleliving.org

Center for a New American Dream
An organization that helps Americans consume responsibly to protect
the environment, enhance quality of life, and promote social justice.
www.newdream.org

The Simple Living Network
An organization that promotes "simplicity circles" to help people
simplify their lives
www.simpleliving.net/studygroups

RMIT University (Australia)
A site that publicizes research on "anti-consumption," including a
page that re-imagines the Australian suburb.
www.rmit.edu.au/anticonsumerism

ECOLOGICAL ECONOMICS

The Gund Institute for Ecological Economics
A research organization at the University of Vermont that focuses on
creating sustainable economies.
www.uvm.edu/giee

The International Society for Ecological Economics
An organization that advances the study of ecological economics and
publishes the journal *Ecological Economics*
www.ecoeco.org

ENERGY, CLIMATE, AND TRANSPORTATION

Evangelical Climate Initiative
A site with information on the climate-related "Call to Action" issued
by more than 85 evangelical leaders.
www.christiansandclimate.org

Interfaith Coalition on Energy
An organization offering technical assistance on energy issues to houses of worship in the Philadelphia area.
www.interfaithenergy.com

Interfaith Climate Change Network
The site of the Interfaith Climate and Energy Campaigns of the National Council of Churches.
www.protectingcreation.org

Interfaith Power and Light (The Regeneration Project)
An organization that helps houses of worship reduce energy use and advocate for greener energy and climate policies.
www.theregenerationproject.org/ipl

What Would Jesus Drive? Campaign
An educational campaign that reflects on the problems associated with transportation from a Christian perspective.
www.whatwouldjesusdrive.org

Notes

Introduction

1. W.H. Auden and L. Kronenberger, *The Viking Book of Aphorisms* (New York: Viking Press, 1966).

2. Tony Deamer, e-mail to author, 26 March 2006, and conversation with author, 27 March 2006.

3. Bahá'í Topics, "Baha'u'llah: His Teachings," at http://info.bahai.org /bahaullah-teachings.html, viewed 3 April 2006.

4. Deamer, op. cit. note 2.

5. Anil Ananthaswamy, "Earth Faces Sixth Mass Extinction," *New Scientist*, 18 March 2004.

6. Michael Renner, *Ending Violent Conflict*, Worldwatch Paper 146 (Washington, DC: Worldwatch Institute, April 1999).

7. Sojourners, "The Seven Deadly Social Sins Poster," at www.sojo.net/ index.cfm?action=resources.catalog&mode=display_detail&ResourceID=126, viewed 27 April 2006.

8. Thomas Berry, *The Great Work* (New York: Bell Tower, 1999), p. 52.

9. Ibid., pp. 67–68.

10. World Commission on Environment and Development, *Our Common Future* (Oxford: Oxford University Press, 1988).

11. Jay McDaniel, "Spirituality and Sustainability," *Conservation Biology*, December 2002, p. 1461.

12. Max Oelschlaeger, *Caring for Creation* (New Haven: Yale University Press, 1994), pp. 11–12.

13. Ibid., p. 12.

14. Thomas Moore, "Religion," in Marianne Williamson and Anne Lamott, *Imagine: What America Could Be in the 21st Century* (New York: Rodale Books, 2000).

15. Mary Evelyn Tucker, *Worldly Wonder: Religions Enter Their Ecological Phase* (Chicago: Open Court, 2002), p. 36.

16. Janet L. Sawin, "Charting a New Energy Future," in Worldwatch Institute, *State of the World 2003* (New York: W.W. Norton & Company, 2003), p. 98.

Chapter 1. The Power of Vision: Worldviews Shape Progress

1. Richard Eckersley, "Running on Empty," *The Australian Financial Review*, 29 January 1999.

2. Reverend Dave Bookless, Executive Director, A Rocha UK, Southall, Middlesex, United Kingdom, interview with author, 15 April 2005.

3. Ibid.

4. Ibid.

5. "Worldviews; Understanding Our Place in a Global Age," in Richard C. Foltz, *Worldviews, Religion, and the Environment: A Global Anthology* (Belmont, CA: Wadsworth Publishing, 2003), p. 2.

6. Sidebar 1–1 from the following sources: Lynn White, "The Historical Roots of Our Ecological Crisis," in Roger S. Gottlieb, *This Sacred Earth: Religion, Nature, Environment* (New York: Routledge, 1996), pp. 184–93; critique of White from J. Baird Callicott, "Genesis and John Muir," *ReVision*, Winter 1990, pp. 31–46; Carl Pope, Executive Director, Sierra Club, remarks at Symposium on Religion, Science, and the Environment, Santa Barbara, CA, 6–8 November 1997; St. Francis from White, op. cit. this note, pp. 192–93.

7. Huston Smith, *Why Religion Matters: The Fate of the Human Spirit in an Age of Disbelief* (New York: HarperSanFrancisco, 2001), p. 11.

8. Mary Midgley, *The Myths We Live By* (London: Routledge, 2003), p. 14.

9. Ibid.

10. Tu Weiming, "Beyond the Enlightenment Mentality," in Mary Evelyn Tucker and John Berthrong, eds., *Confucianism and Ecology: The Interrelation of Heaven, Earth, and Humans* (Cambridge, MA: Center for the Study of World Religions, Harvard Divinity School, 1998), p. 21.

11. Ibid.

12. Thomas Moore, "Religion," in Marianne Williamson and Anne Lamott,

Imagine: What America Could Be in the 21st Century (New York: Rodale Books, 2000).

13. United Nations Environment Programme, "The Nitrogen Cascade: Impacts of Food and Energy Production on the Global Nitrogen Cycle," *Global Environmental Outlook Year Book 2003* (Nairobi: 2003).

14. Shiva quoted in Pat Howard, "The Confrontation of Modern and Traditional Knowledge Systems in Development," *Canadian Journal of Communication*, Vol. 19, No. 2 (1994).

15. Vandana Shiva, *Staying Alive* (London: Zed Books, 1989), p. 24.

16. Ibid.

17. Ibid., p. 22.

18. Carol Jorgenson, Director, American Indian Environmental Office, U.S. Environmental Protection Agency, remarks at Panel Discussion at the Interfaith Symposium for Our Common Future, Georgetown University, Washington, DC, 1 April 2005.

19. Howard, op. cit. note 14.

20. Ibid.

21. Tu, op. cit. note 10, p. 24.

22. Societal drivers from Thomas Berry, *The Great Work* (New York: Bell Tower, 1999); individual drivers from Gerald T. Gardner and Paul C. Stern, *Environmental Problems and Human Behavior* (Boston: Allyn and Bacon, 1996), pp. 21–32; Nestle from Robin Broad and John Cavanagh, "The Corporate Accountability Movement: Lessons and Opportunities," A Study for the World Wildlife Fund's Project on International Financial Flows and the Environment (Washington, DC: 1998), pp. 12, 30.

Chapter 2. The Paradox of Progress in the 20th Century

1. John Barlett, *Bartlett's Familiar Quotations*, 16th edition (Boston: Little, Brown and Company, 1992), p. 685.

2. U.S. Centers for Disease Control and Prevention, "Fact Sheet: Life Expectancy Reaches Record High" (Atlanta, GA: 28 February 2005).

3. S. Jay Olshansky et al., "A Potential Decline in Life Expectancy in the United States in the 21st Century," *The New England Journal of Medicine*, 17 March 2005, pp. 1138–45.

4. Sidebar 2–1 from the following sources: European energy use from John Goyder, *Technology and Society: A Canadian Perspective* (Peterborough, ON:

Broadview Press, 1997), p. 15; tens of thousands and before World War I
from National Academy of Engineering, "High Performance Materials History
Part 5—Composites," at www.greatachievements.org/?id=3817, viewed 16
May 2005; 92 elements from U.S. Congress, Office of Technology Assessment,
Green Products By Design: Choices for a Cleaner Environment (Washington, DC:
U.S. Government Printing Office, September 1992), p. 26; scientific journals
from Rudi Volti, *Society and Technological Change* (New York: St. Martin's Press,
1995), p. 258; Hershey H. Friedman, "The Obsolescence of Academic
Departments," *Radical Pedagogy*, Fall 2001.

5. Table 2–1 from the following sources: 1st through 19th centuries from
Michael Renner, *Ending Violent Conflict*, Worldwatch Paper 146 (Washington,
DC: Worldwatch Institute, April 1999), p. 10; 20th century from Milton
Leitenburg, "Deaths in Wars and Conflicts Between 1945 and 2000," paper
prepared for Conference on Data Collection in Armed Conflict, Uppsala,
Sweden, 8–9 June 2001; 20th century population data from U.S. Census
Bureau, International Data Base, "World Population, 1950-2050" and "Histor-
ical Estimates of World Population," www.census.gov/ipc/www/world.html,
viewed 4 May 2006.

6. Renner, ibid., p. 10.

7. Ibid., pp. 11–12.

8. Ibid., p. 13.

9. Ibid., p. 14.

10. "Rwanda: How the Genocide Happened," *BBC News*, 1 April 2004.

11. Bill McKibben, "A Special Moment in History," *Atlantic Monthly*, May 1998.

12. Table 2–2 from the following: mass extinction from Philip S. Levin and
Donald Levin, "The Real Biodiversity Crisis," *American Scientist*, January–
February 2002, p. 6; extinction rates from Millennium Ecosystem Assessment
(MA), *Ecosystems and Human Well-Being: A Framework for Assessment*
(Washington, DC: Island Press, 2005), p. 4; vertebrates from Jonathan Loh
and Mathis Wackernagel, eds., "Living Planet Report 2004" (Gland, Switzer-
land: WWF, October 2004), p. 1; temperature from Goddard Institute for
Space Studies, "Global Temperature Anomalies in .01 C," http://data.giss.nasa
.gov/gistemp/tabledata/GLB.Ts.txt, viewed 9 May 2006; human influence
from Intergovernmental Panel on Climate Change, *IPCC Second Assessment
Report–Climate Change 1995* (Geneva: 1995); sources from A.P.M. Baede et al.,
"Human Induced Climate Variations," in *Climate Change 2001: The Scientific
Basis* (Geneva: Intergovernmental Panel on Climate Change, 2001), p. 92;
greenhouse gases from Randolph E. Schmid, "Effect of Greenhouse Gases
Rising, Government Says," *Environmental News Network*, 28 September 2005;
half of original forest area from Dirk Bryant, "The Last Frontier Forests"

(Washington, DC: World Resources Institute, 1997), p. 43; Brazil from "Worse-than-anticipated Deforestation Jolts Brazil," *EcoAmericas*, June 2005; rivers from Sandra Postel, *Liquid Assets: The Critical Need to Safeguard Freshwater Ecosystems*, Worldwatch Paper 170 (Washington, DC: Worldwatch Institute, July 2005), p. 16; groundwater from Lester R. Brown, *Plan B: Rescuing a Planet Under Stress and a Civilization in Trouble* (New York: W.W. Norton & Company, 2006), pp. 42–43; human share from Sandra L. Postel, Gretchen C. Daly, and Paul R. Ehrlich, "Human Appropriation of Renewable Fresh Water," *Science*, 9 February 1996, pp. 785–88; large dams from Sandra Postel and Amy Vickers, "Boosting Water Productivity," in Worldwatch Institute, *State of the World 2004* (New York: W.W. Norton & Company, 2004), pp. 46–47; fish stocks from U.N. Food and Agriculture Organization (FAO), "Depleted Fish Stocks Require Recovery Efforts," press release (Rome: 7 March 2005); coral reefs from Clive Wilkinson, ed., *Status of Coral Reefs of the World 2004* (Townsville, Queensland: Australian Institute of Marine Science, 2004), pp. 7, 10.

13. MA, ibid., p. 1.

14. Ibid.

15. Geoffrey Howard, "Invasive Species and Wetlands," outline of a keynote presentation to the 7th Conference of the Contracting Parties to the Convention on Wetlands, San José, Costa Rica, May 1999.

16. National Academies Press, *Abrupt Climate Change: Inevitable Surprises* (Washington, DC: 2002), p. 107.

17. Global Footprint Network, "Results Page (hectare version)," www.foot printnetwork.org/gfn_sub.php?content=footprint_hectares, viewed 7 May 2006.

18. Table 2–3 from Global Footprint Network, "National Footprint and Biocapacity Accounts, 2005 edition," at www.footprintnetwork.org, viewed 4 May 2006.

19. Figure 2–1 from Global Footprint Network, "Humanity's Footprint, 1961–2002," at www.footprintnetwork.org/gfn_sub.php?content=global_ footprint, viewed 28 December 2005.

20. Figure 2–2 from Angus Maddison, "World Population, GDP, and per capita GDP, 1-2003 AD," at www.ggdc.net/maddison, viewed 7 May 2006.

21. World Bank, *World Development Report 2006* (Washington, DC: 2006), p. 55.

22. World Bank, *World Development Report 2000/2001* (New York: Oxford University Press, 2001), p. 51.

23. Total compensation, with stock options, from Louis Lavelle, Frederick F.

Jesperson, and Michael Arndt, "Executive Pay," *Business Week Online*, 15 April 2002; 350 times is a Worldwatch calculation based on executive pay data from Towers Perrin, "Total Remuneration—Chief Executive Officer," at www.towers.com and on worker pay from "Hourly Direct Pay in U.S. Dollars for Production Workers in Manufacturing, 30 Countries or Areas, 1975–2001," in U.S. Bureau of Labor Statistics, "International Comparisons of Hourly Compensation Costs for Production Workers in Manufacturing, 1975–2001," press release (Washington, DC: 27 September 2002); fivefold from Scott Klinger et al., *Executive Excess 2002: CEOs Cook the Books, Skewer the Rest of Us*, Ninth Annual CEO Compensation Survey (Washington, DC: Institute for Policy Studies and United for a Fair Economy, August 2002).

24. United Nations Development Programme, *Human Development Report 1998* (New York: 1998), p. 30.

25. FAO, "FAO Reports A Setback in the War Against Hunger," press release (Rome: 25 November 2003).

26. World Bank, *World Development Indicators 2002* (Washington, DC: 2002), p. 124.

27. Fossil fuel use from Janet L. Sawin, "Fossil Fuel Use Up," in Worldwatch Institute, *Vital Signs 2003* (New York: W.W. Norton & Company, 2003), pp. 34–35.

28. Payal Sampat, "Scrapping Mining Dependence," in Worldwatch Institute, *State of the World 2003* (New York: W.W. Norton & Company, 2003), p. 113.

29. Ibid.

30. Jason Venetoulis, Dahlia Chazan, and Christopher Gaudet, "Ecological Footprint of Nations 2004" (Oakland, CA: Redefining Progress, March 2004) p. 12.

31. World Bank, op. cit. note 21, pp. 55–69.

32. Murray Scot Tanner, "We the People (of China)…," *Wall Street Journal*, 2 February 2006.

33. Dennis Meadows, "Dennis Meadows One on One: Growth on a Finite Planet," video (Waltham, MA: Pegasus Communications, 2005). See also Donella H. Meadows, Dennis L. Meadows, and Jorgen Randers, *Beyond the Limits: Confronting Global Collapse, Envisioning a Sustainable Future* (White River Junction, VT: Chelsea Green Publishing, 1992).

34. Ibid.

35. Ibid.

36. Donella H. Meadows, Dennis L. Meadows, and Jorgen Randers, "Beyond the Limits to Growth," *In Context*, Summer 1992, p. 10.

Chapter 3. Tools for Course Correction: Religions' Contributions

1. Mahatma Gandhi Foundation, The Official Mahatma Gandhi eArchive and Reference Library, "Quotes," at www.mahatma.org.in/quotes/quotes.jsp ?link=qt, viewed 1 May 2006.

2. Malcolm Brown and Shirley Seaton, *Christmas Truce: The Western Front, December 1914* (London: Pan Books, 1999).

3. Stanley Weintraub, *Silent Night: The Story of the World War I Christmas Truce* (New York: The Free Press, 2001).

4. Reverend Dave Bookless, Executive Director, A Rocha UK, Southall, Middlesex, United Kingdom, interview with author, 15 April 2005.

5. Mathieu Deflem, "Ritual, Anti-Structure, and Religion: A Discussion of Victor Turner's Processual Symbolic Analysis," *Journal for the Scientific Study of Religion*, Vol. 30, No. 1 (1991), pp. 1–25; Robert Bellah, "Civil Religion in America," *Daedalus*, Vol. 96 (1967), pp. 1–21. Sidebar 3–1 based on the following: Jewish Virtual Library, "Ner Namid," at www.jewishvirtuallibrary .org/jsource/Judaism/ner_tamid.html, viewed 13 December 2005; Rabbi Fred Dobbs, Adat Shalom Reconstructionist Congregation, Bethesda, MD, inter-view with author, 4 November 2005; Adat Shalom Web site, www.adatshalom .net, viewed 13 December 2005.

6. E.N. Anderson, *Ecologies of the Heart: Emotion, Belief, and the Environment* (New York: Oxford University Press, 1996), p. 166.

7. Ibid.

8. John A. Grim, ed., *Indigenous Traditions and Ecology: The Interbeing of Cosmology and Community* (Cambridge, MA: Harvard University Press, 2001).

9. Anderson, op. cit. note 6.

10. Rabbi Goldie Milgram, "Eco-Kosher: Jewish Spirituality in Action," at www.rebgoldie.com/eco-kosher.html, viewed 6 December 2005.

11. Susan M. Darlington, "Practical Spirituality and Community Forests: Monks, Ritual, and Radical Conservatism in Thailand," in Anna L. Tsing and Paul Greenough, eds., *Nature in the Global South* (Durham, NC: Duke University Press, 2003).

12. Rabbi Fred Dobbs, Adat Shalom Reconstructionist Congregation, Bethesda, MD, conversation with author, 4 November 2005; Rabbi Fred

Dobbs, Adat Shalom Reconstructionist Congregation, Bethesda, MD, e-mail to author, 2 February 2006.

13. Stalin quoted in Winston Churchill, *The Second World War: The Gathering Storm* (Boston: Houghton Mifflin, 1948), p. 601; Poland from Carl Bernstein and Marco Politi, *His Holiness: John Paul II and the History of Our Time* (New York: Penguin Books, 1996), pp. 11–12; Tibet from "UN Rights Chief Pressures Boy on Panchen Lama," *Agence France Presse*, 19 August 2002.

14. Churches for Middle East Peace, "U.S. Church Leaders Urge U.S. to Avoid Military Action Against Iraq," press release (Washington, DC: 12 September 2002).

15. Joe Feuerherd, "Papal Envoy, President Dialogue and Disagree," *National Catholic Reporter*, 14 March 2003.

16. National Council of Churches, "NCC 2002 General Assembly Calls on President Bush, Congress to 'Do All Possible, Without Going to War' to Resolve the Iraq Crisis," press release (New York: 16 November 2002).

17. The Pew Research Center for the People and the Press, "Different Faiths, Different Messages: Americans Hearing About Iraq From The Pulpit, But Religious Faith Not Defining Opinions," survey report (Washington, DC: 19 March 2003).

18. David Barrett and Todd Johnson, *World Christian Trends, AD 30—AD 2200* (Pasadena, CA: William Carey Library, 2001). Table 3–1 based on the following: Adherents.com, "Major Religions of the World Ranked by Number of Adherents," www.adherents.com/Religions_By_Adherents.html; population data from U.S. Census Bureau, International Data Base, www.census.gov/ipc/www/idbnew.html, viewed 7 December 2005.

19. Religious adherence statistics from Adherents.com, "Predominant Religions," www.adherents.com/adh_predom.html, viewed 7 May 2006.

20. The World Conservation Union (IUCN), "The Pakistan National Conservation Strategy" (Karachi: 1991); IUCN, "Final Report, Mid-term Review of National Conservation Strategy: Mass Awareness Initiatives" (Islamabad: 2000).

21. Grim, op. cit. note 8.

22. Belden, Russonello & Stewart, Research and Communications, "Americans and Biodiversity: New Perspectives in 2002," report prepared for The Biodiversity Project (Washington, DC: February 2002), p. 3. The most common response, "to preserve the environment for our children," was mentioned by 58 percent of respondents.

23. James Wolfensohn, "Foreword," in Martin Palmer with Victoria Finlay, *Faith in Conservation* (Washington, DC: World Bank, 2003), p. xi.

24. Mosques from IUCN, "Final Report...," op. cit. note 20.

25. Catholic health systems from Catholic Charities USA, "Frequently Asked Questions," at www.catholiccharitiesusa.org/about/faqs.cfm

26. Interfaith Center on Corporate Responsibility Web site, at www.iccr.org.

27. Ibid.

28. Tracey Rembert, Coordinator of Shareholder Advocacy Programs, Shareholder Action Network, Washington, DC, conversation with author, 15 May 2002.

29. Ismail Serageldin and Christian Grootaert, "Defining Social Capital: An Integrating View," in Partha Dagupta and Ismail Serageldin, eds., *Social Capital: A Multi-faceted Perspective* (Washington, DC: World Bank, 2000).

30. Andrew Greeley, "Coleman Revisited: Religious Structures as a Source of Social Capital," *American Behavioral Scientist*, March/April 1997, p. 591.

Chapter 4. New Vision: Nature, Then Economies

1. Rose Marie Berger, "Heaven in Henry County," *Sojourners*, July 2004.

2. Rosita Worl, President, Sealaska Heritage Institute, Juneau, AK, conversation with author, 13 April 2006.

3. Ibid.

4. Ibid.

5. Michelle L. Bell and Devra Lee Davis, "Reassessment of the Lethal London Fog of 1952: Novel Indicators of Acute and Chronic Consequences of Acute Exposure to Air Pollution, *Environmental Health Perspectives*, June 2001, pp. 389–94; Loretta Neal, "Burned Into History: The Cuyahoga River Fires," *Balanced Living Magazine*, July–August 2005.

6. Association for the Study of Peak Oil Web site, www.peakoil.net, viewed 16 May 2006; International Food Policy Research Institute and WorldFish Center, "Outlook for Fish to 2020: Meeting Global Demand" (Washington, DC: 2 October 2003); "Web Focus: Global Water Crisis," *Nature*, www.nature.com/nature/focus/water/index.html, viewed 16 May 2006.

7. Matthew Waite and Craig Pittman, "Katrina Offers Lesson on Wetlands Protection," *St. Petersburg Times*, 5 September 2005.

8. Steven L. Buchmann and Gary Paul Nabhan, *The Forgotten Pollinators* (Washington, DC: Island Press, 1996).

9. Robert Costanza et al., "The Value of the World's Ecosystem Services and Natural Capital," *Nature*, 15 May 1997, p. 256.

10. Peter M. Vitousek et al., "Human Appropriation of the Products of Photosynthesis," *BioScience*, June 1986, pp. 368–73.

11. Sandra L. Postel, Gretchen C. Daily, and Paul R. Ehrlich, "Human Appropriation of Renewable Fresh Water," *Science*, 9 February 1996, pp. 785–88.

12. Gary Gardner, Erik Assadourian, and Radhika Sarin, "The State of Consumption Today," in Worldwatch Institute, *State of the World 2004* (New York: W.W. Norton & Company, 2004), pp. 3–21.

13. Fourfold from Ernst von Weisäcker, Amory Lovins, and Hunter Lovins, *Factor Four: Doubling Wealth, Halving Resource Use* (London: Earthscan, 1997); tenfold from Friends of the Earth Europe, *Towards Sustainable Europe* (Brussels: 1995); Friedrich Schmidt-Bleek, "MIPS and Factor 10 for a Sustainable and Profitable Economy" (Wuppertal: Wuppertal Institute, 1997).

14. European Commission, "Directive 2000/53/EC of the European Parliament and of the Council of 18 September on end-of-life vehicles," *Official Journal of the European Communities*, 10 October 2000.

15. Stuart L. Hart, *Capitalism at the Crossroads: The Unlimited Business Opportunities in Solving the World's Most Difficult Problems* (Philadelphia: Wharton School Publishing, 2005).

16. Institute for Manufacturing, University of Cambridge, "Case Number 8: Interface Evergreen Carpet Lease System" (Cambridge, UK: 9 December 2003).

17. CarSharing.net Web site, at www.carsharing.net, viewed 1 May 2006; European car sharing Web site, at www.carsharing.org, viewed 1 May 2006.

18. John Ehrenfeld and Nicolas Gertler, "Industrial Ecology in Practice: The Evolution of Interdependence at Kalundborg," *Journal of Industrial Ecology*, Vol. 1, No. 1 (1997).

19. E. F. Schumacher, "Buddhist Economics," *Parabola*, Spring 1991, pp. 63–39.

20. M.M. Metwally, "Economic Consequences of Applying Islamic Principles in Muslim Societies," *International Journal of Social Economics*, September 1997, pp. 941–57.

21. Glen Alexandrin, "Elements of Buddhist Economics," *International Journal of Social Economics*, Vol. 20, No. 2 (1993), p. 5.

22. Sallie McFague, *Life Abundant: Rethinking Theology and Economy for a Planet in Peril* (Minneapolis, MN: Fortress Press, 1991), pp. 119–20.

Chapter 5. Nature as Sacred Ground

1.   "John Muir Quotes," www.brainyquote.com/quotes/quotes/j/johnmuir 104245.html, viewed 9 May 2006.

2. Martin Palmer, Secretary General, Alliance of Religions and Conservation (ARC), Kelston Park, Bath, United Kingdom, conversation with author, 9 January 2006.

3. Ibid.

4. Ibid.

5. Sidebar 5–1 from Mary Evelyn Tucker and John Grim, "Series Foreword," in Christopher Key Chapple and Mary Evelyn Tucker, *Hinduism and Ecology* (Cambridge, MA: Harvard University Press, 2000), pp. xxv–xxvii.

6. Mary Evelyn Tucker, *Worldly Wonder: Religions Enter Their Ecological Phase* (Chicago: Open Court, 2002), pp. 36–54.

7. David G. Hallman, Climate Change Programme Coordinator, World Council of Churches, Geneva, Switzerland, conversation with author, 21 March 2006.

8. National Council of Churches, "Subject Index of Anthology of Environmental Statements," at www.nccecojustice.org/anthoindex.htm, viewed 17 April 2004.

9. Sidebar 5–2 from Sister Diane Cundiff, Principal, Colegio Santa Maria, São Paulo, Brazil, conversation with author, 10 May 2005.

10. Worldwatch estimate based on Coalition on the Environment and Jewish Life, "Seeds," www.coejl.org/programbank/viewprog.php, viewed 4 May 2006.

11. Islamic Foundation for Ecology and Environmental Sciences Web site, at www.ifees.org, viewed 5 June 2006.

12. What Would Jesus Drive?, "Jim's Tour Journal," at www.whatwouldjesus drive.org/journal, viewed 2 May 2006.

13. Symposia from Maria Becket, Coordinator, Religion, Science, and the Environment (RSE) Symposium, conversation with author, 25 September 2002; other details from RSE Web site, www.rsesymposia.org, viewed 2 May 2006.

14. Laurence David Mee, "The Black Sea Today," paper prepared for RSE Symposium II: Black Sea 1997: "The Black Sea in Crisis," available at www.rsesym posia.org/page.asp?p=35, viewed 4 May 2006.

15. RSE, "Presentations," www.rsesymposia.org/page.asp?p=39, viewed 4 May 2006.

16. John Chryssavgis, "Conference Report: A Symposium on the Danube: Religion and Science in Dialogue about the Environment," *Worldviews*, Vol. 4 (2000), p. 82.

17. Philip Weller, former Program Director, WWF, conversation with author, 20 September 2002; Patriarch's involvement from Jasmina Bachmann, International Commission for the Protection of the Danube River, Vienna, Austria, conversation with author, 23 September 2002.

18. ARC, "Living Churchyards," at www.arcworld.org/projects.asp?projectID =76, viewed 17 April 2006.

19. Select Committee on Environment, Transport and Regional Affairs, United Kingdom Parliament, "Memorandum by the Living Churchyard & Cemetery Project (CEM 60)," at www.publications.parliament.uk/pa/cm200001/cmse lect/cmenvtra/91/91m66.htm, viewed 4 May 2006.

20. Palmer, op. cit. note 2.

21. Bill Bradlee, Managing Director, The Regeneration Project, San Francisco, CA, e-mail to author, 25 April 2006.

22. Table 5–1 from the following sources: Michigan Interfaith Power and Light Web site, at www.miipl.org, viewed 3 January 2005; The Regeneration Project/Interfaith Power and Light National Campaign, "Report to the Surdna Foundation" (San Francisco: 31 August 2005).

23. Sally Bingham, Executive Director, The Regeneration Project, San Francisco, CA, conversation with author, 16 November 2005.

24. Andrew Rudin, Project Coordinator, Interfaith Coalition on Energy, Philadelphia, PA, conversation with author, 22 December 2005.

25. Andrew Rudin, "Blessed Are They Who Turn Things Off," *Earth Letter*, undated, p. 10.

26. U.S. Environmental Protection Agency (EPA), Energy Star Program "Congregations," at www.energystar.gov/index.cfm?c=small_business.sb_congre gations, viewed 4 May 2006.

27. Ibid.

28. Ibid.

29. Bruce Barcott, "For God So Loved the World," *Outside*, March 2001.

30. The Noah Alliance Web site, at www.noahalliance.org, viewed 3 May 2006.

31. "GreenFaith Testifies in Support of Classifying CO2 as a Pollutant," *Partners: Interfaith Perspectives on the Environment*, Spring 2005.

32. "GreenFaith Joins Lawsuit to Clean Up Newark Bay," *Partners: Interfaith Perspectives on the Environment*, Spring 2005.

33. "GreenFaith Seeks Partners to Fight Dirty Diesel," *Partners: Interfaith Perspectives on the Environment*, Winter 2006.

34. Tom Gibb, "The Nun Who Died for the Amazon," *BBC News*, 15 December 2005.

Chapter 6. Warming to the Climate Challenge

1. World Meteorological Organization, United Nations Environment Programme (UNEP), and Environment Canada, statement at The Changing Atmosphere: Implications for Global Security Conference, Toronto, Ontario, Canada, June 1988.

2. Allison Caldwell, "The World Today—Vanuatu Village Relocated Due to Rising Sea Level," *Australian Broadcasting Corporation*, 6 December 2005.

3. UNEP, "Pacific Island Villagers First Climate Change 'Refugees,'" press release (Nairobi: 6 December 2005).

4. Caldwell, op. cit. note 2.

5. Brian Phillips, Coordinator, Capacity Building to Enable the Development of Adaptation Measures in Pacific Island Countries (CBDAMPIC), interview with author, 7 March 2006.

6. Estimate of 2–3 meters from UNEP, op. cit. note 3; 50 meters from Hannington Alatoa, Ombudsman of the Government of Vanuatu, keynote address to the "Creating a Climate for Change: CUSO Communities and the Impact of Climate Change" conference, Winnipeg, Manitoba, Canada, 19–24 March 2004.

7. Pacific Regional Environmental Programme, "Innovations in Adapting to Climate Change," in *2003 Annual Report* (Apia, Samoa: 2004).

8. Caldwell, op. cit. note 2.

9. Pan American Health Organization, "Impact of Hurricane Mitch on Central America," *Epidemiological Bulletin*, December 1998, p. 2.

10. Sir John Houghton, "Climate Change: A Christian Challenge and Opportunity," presentation to a meeting of the National Association of Evangelicals, Washington, DC, March 2005.

11. National Climatic Data Center, U.S. National Oceanic and Atmospheric Administration, "Flooding in China, Summer 1998," at http://lwf.ncdc.noaa.gov/oa/reports/chinaflooding/chinaflooding.html, viewed 28 March 2006.

12. Andrew Simms, John Magrath, and Hannah Reid, "Up in Smoke: Threats From, and Responses to, the Impact of Global Warming on Human Development" (London: New Economics Foundation and International Institute for

Environment and Development, October 2004), p. 5.

13. Ibid., p. 8.

14. Ibid., p. 7.

15. Shaoni Battacharya, "European Heatwave Causes 35,000 Deaths," *New Scientist*, 23 October 2003.

16. David G. Hallman, Climate Change Programme Coordinator, World Council of Churches, Geneva, Switzerland, interview with author, 21 March 2006.

17. Ibid.

18. David G. Hallman, "Report on the 11th Session of the Conference of the Parties to the UN Framework Convention on Climate Change and the 1st Session of the Meeting of the Parties to the Kyoto Protocol COP11/MOP1, November 28 to December 9, 2005" (Geneva: World Council of Churches, 2005).

19. Sidebar 6–1 from ibid.

20. Ibid.

21. International Federation of Red Cross and Red Crescent Societies (IFRC), *World Disasters Report 2002* (Geneva: 2002).

22. Ibid.; population increase from U.S. Census Bureau, International Data Base, www.census.gov/cgi-bin/ipc/idbsprd, viewed 3 May 2006.

23. Hallman, op. cit. note 16.

24. Bruce Barcott, "For God So Loved the World," *Outside*, March 2001.

25. Table 6–1 based on the following sources: EEN activities in 1990s from Paul O'Donnell, "The Call to Conservation," *Science and Spirit*, May–June 2006; "Oxford Declaration on Global Warming: Climate scientists and Christian leaders call for action," prepared at Forum 2002: Climate Change, St. Anne's College, Oxford University, 14–17 July 2002, available at www.climateforum2002.org/statement.cfm; What Would Jesus Drive? Web site, at http://whatwouldjesusdrive.org, viewed 3 May 2006; Jim Ball, Executive Director, Evangelical Environmental Network, Washington, DC, interview with author, 15 April 2005; Sandy Cove Covenant from Evangelical Climate Initiative, "Evangelical Climate Initiative: A History," www.christiansand climate.org/pub/eci_history.pdf, viewed 3 May 2006; National Association of Evangelicals, "For the Health of the Nation: An Evangelical Call to Civic Responsibility," at www.nae.net/images/civic_responsibility2.pdf, viewed 3 April 2006; Evangelical Climate Initiative, "Climate Change: An Evangelical Call to Action," at www.christiansandclimate.org/statement, viewed 2 May 2006.

26. Evangelical Climate Initiative, "Climate Change: An Evangelical Call to Action," ibid.

27. Sheryl Anderson Blunt, "The New Climate Coalition," *Christianity Today*, 8 February 2006.

28. Matthew Anderson-Stembridge, Program Director, Interfaith Climate and Energy Campaign, Washington, DC, conversation with author, 31 January 2006 and e-mail to author, 19 April 2006.

29. Ibid.

30. Brad Knickerbocker, "Forces of Faith Enter Fray over Energy Policy," *Christian Science Monitor*, 27 February 2002.

31. Worldwatch calculation based on data in "An Interfaith Initiative on Behalf of the States' Citizens: Pennsylvania Sustainable Energy Charter," in Interfaith Climate and Energy Campaign, "A Faithful Vision for Future Energy: Interfaith Climate and Energy State Charters" (Washington, DC: February 2006).

32. Ibid.

33. Joy Bergey, Pennsylvania Interfaith Climate Change Campaign, conversation with author, 21 March 2006 and e-mail to author, 18 April 2006.

34. "An Interfaith Initiative on Behalf of the States' Citizens: Pennsylvania Sustainable Energy Charter," op. cit. note 31.

35. Bergey, e-mail to author, op. cit. note 33.

36. Bergey, conversation with author, op. cit. note 33.

37. Ibid.

38. Andy Burt, Maine Interfaith Climate and Energy Initiative, conversations with author, 8 March 2006 and 28 April 2006.

39. Ibid.

40. Ibid.

41. Ibid.

42. Ibid.

43. Ibid.

44. Ibid.

45. Ibid.

46. Ibid.

47. Ibid.

Chapter 7. New Vision: Choosing Well-Being

1. The Quotations Page, "Quotation Details, at www.quotationspage.com/quote/38128.html, viewed 2 May 2006.

2. Gunter Pauli, Zero Emissions Research and Initiatives, "The Paradigm Shifted: The Renaissance of the Rainforest," article for *ReSurgence*, Summer 2005, available at www.zeri.org.

3. Figure 7–1 from David G. Myers, *The American Paradox: Spiritual Hunger in an Age of Plenty* (New Haven: Yale Nota Bene, 2001), p. 137, with updates from David G. Myers, Hope College, Holland, MI, e-mail to Erik Assadourian, Worldwatch Institute, 20 October 2003.

4. Ibid., p. 5.

5. Ronald Inglehart and Hans-Dieter Klingemann, "Genes, Culture, Democracy, and Happiness," in E. Diener and E. M. Suh, eds., *Culture and Subjective Well-Being* (Cambridge, MA: MIT Press, 2000), p. 171.

6. Dennis Meadows, "Dennis Meadows One on One: Growth on a Finite Planet," video (Waltham, MA: Pegasus Communications, 2005).

7. Adapted from Millennium Ecosystem Assessment (MA), *Ecosystems and Human Wellbeing: A Framework for Assessment* (Washington, DC: Island Press, 2005).

8. Canada from Mike Nickerson, 2006 Green Party candidate, Ontario, Canada, conversation with author, 6 January 2006.

9. MA, op. cit. note 7.

10. Robert Prescott-Allen, *The Wellbeing of Nations: A Country-by-Country Index of Quality of Life and the Environment* (Washington, DC: Island Press: 2001).

11. Datamonitor, "Simplicity," report brochure (New York: May 2003).

12. Organic Centre Wales, "Certified and policy-supported organic and in-conversion land area in Europe," www.organic.aber.ac.uk/statistics/euroarea05.htm, viewed 2 June 2006.

13. LOHAS, "About LOHAS," awww.lohas.com/about.htm, viewed 2 May 2006.

14. Robert D. Putnam, *Bowling Alone: The Collapse and Revival of American Community* (New York: Simon and Schuster, 2000), p. 332.

15. Graham Meltzer, "Cohousing: Verifying the Importance of Community in the Application of Environmentalism," *Journal of Architectural and Planning*

Research, Vol. 17 (2000), pp. 110–32.

16. Worldwatch calculation based on data in Bureau of Transportation Statistics, U.S. Department of Transportation, "Omnibus Household Survey Shows Americans' Average Commuting Time is Just Over 26 Minutes," press release (Washington, DC: 8 September 2003).

17. Kate Zernike, "Fight Against Fat Shifts to the Workplace," *New York Times*, 12 October 2003.

18. Anders Hayden, "Europe's Work-Time Alternatives," in John de Graaf, ed., *Take Back Your Time* (San Francisco: Berrett Koehler, 2003), pp. 202–10.

19. World Bank, "Participatory Budgeting in Brazil," project commissioned by the World Bank Poverty Reduction Group (Washington, DC: undated).

20. Sarvodaya Web site, www.sarvodaya.org, viewed 2 May 2006.

21. D.J. Mitchell, "Sarvodaya: An Introduction to the Sarvodaya Shramadana Movement in Sri Lanka," informational brochure (Moratuwa, Sri Lanka; undated), p. 3.

22. Peñalosa quote from Susan Ives, "The Politics of Happiness," *YES! The Journal of Positive Futures*, Summer 2003, pp. 36–37. Sidebar 7–1 from the following sources: schools from Woodrow Wilson School of Public and International Affairs, "Former Mayor of Bogotá to Speak on Improvement Models for Third World Cities," press release (Princeton, NJ: 26 November 2001) and from Enrique Peñalosa, e-mail to author, 8 October 2003; murders from Curtis Runyan, "Bogotá Designs Transportation for People, Not Cars," *WRI Features* (Washington, DC: World Resources Institute, February 2003); Ives, op. cit. this note.

Chapter 8. Hungry for More: The Consumption Challenge

1. Vance Packard, *The Waste Makers* (New York: David McKay, 1960).

2. Howard Rheingold, "Look Who's Talking," *Wired*, January 1999.

3. Ibid.

4. Ibid.

5. Gary Cross, *An-All Consuming Century: Why Commercialism Won in Modern America* (New York: Columbia University Press, 2000).

6. David Suzuki with Amanda McConnell, *The Sacred Balance: Rediscovering Our Place in Nature* (Seattle: Mountaineers Books, 2002).

7. Bill McKibben, "Returning God to the Center," in Rodney Clapp, ed., *The Consuming Passion: Christianity and the Consumer Culture* (Downers Grove, IL: InterVarsity Press, 1998), p. 45.

8. David R. Loy, "The Religion of the Market," in Harold Coward and Daniel C. Maguire, eds., *Visions of a New Earth* (Albany: State University of New York Press, 2000), p. 15.

9. Sidebar 8–1 from Gary Gardner, Erik Assadourian, and Radhika Sarin, "The State of Consumption Today," in Worldwatch Institute, *State of the World 2004* (New York: W.W. Norton & Company, 2004), pp. 6–11.

10. McKibben, op. cit. note 7, p. 44.

11. Sidebar 8–2 from Gerald Iversen, National Coordinator, Alternatives for Simple Living, Sioux City, IA, conversation with author, 28 April 2006.

12. Millennium Ecosystem Assessment, *Ecosystems and Human Wellbeing: A Framework for Assessment* (Washington, DC: Island Press, 2005).

13. Roger Levett et al., *A Better Choice of Choice: Quality of Life, Consumption, and Economic Growth* (London: The Fabian Society, 2003), p. 49.

14. Janet Sawin, "Making Better Energy Choices," in Worldwatch Institute, op. cit. note 9, p. 29.

15. Energy use from Sawin, ibid.; water use from Sandra Postel and Amy Vickers, "Boosting Water Productivity," in Worldwatch Institute, op. cit. note 9, pp. 48-49; materials from Gary Gardner and Payal Sampat, *Mind Over Matter: Recasting the Role of Materials in Our Lives*, Worldwatch Paper 144 (Washington, DC: Worldwatch Institute, December 1998).

16. Andrew Rudin, "Efficiency and Conservation: An Interview with Andy Rudin," *Energy and Environment*, Vol. 15, No. 6 (2004), p. 1087.

17. Andrew Rudin, "Energy, Religion, and Lifestyle" (Philadelphia, PA: Interfaith Coalition on Energy, September 1991).

18. Rudin, op. cit. note 16.

19. Sidebar 8–3 from the following sources: Bahá'í Reference Library, "World Peace," http://reference.bahai.org/en/t/bic/SB/sb-13.html#fr5, viewed 3 May 2006; Buddhism, Confucianism, Daoism, and Hinduism from Center for a New American Dream, "Religion and Spirituality," www.affluenza.org/cnad/religion.html, viewed 3 May 2006; Christianity and Judaism from *The New Jerusalem Bible* (New York: Doubleday, 1990); Islam from Islam Set, "Environmental Protection in Islan," www.islamset.com/env/section4.html, viewed 3 May 2006.

20. Richard Rohr, "Giving Up Control in Life's Second Half," *National Catholic Reporter*, 8 February 2002.

21. Richard Rohr, "We Should Ask Why So Few Transformations Happen in Church," *National Catholic Reporter*, 28 March 2003.

22. Gardner, Assadourian, and Sarin, op. cit. note 9, p. 11.

23. Ibid.

24. World Bank, *World Development Report 2006* (Washington, DC: 2006).

25. Rudin, op. cit. note 16, p. 1088.

26. Andrew Rudin, Efficology Web site, at www.efficology.com/energy.htm #appenergy, viewed 6 April 2006.

27. Table 8–1 from the following sources: makeup and perfumes from "Pots of Promise," *The Economist*, 24 May 2003, pp. 69–71; pet food and ice cream from United Nations Development Programme, *Human Development Report 1998* (New York: Oxford University Press, 1998), p. 37; ocean cruises from Lisa Mastny, "Cruise Industry Buoyant," in Worldwatch Institute, *Vital Signs 2002* (New York: W.W. Norton & Company, 2002), p. 122; additional annual investments from Michael Renner, "Military Expenditures on the Rise" and from Erik Assadourian, "Consumption Patterns Contribute to Mortality," both in Worldwatch Institute, *Vital Signs 2003* (New York: W.W. Norton & Company, 2003), pp. 119 and 108.

28. Levett et al., op. cit. note 13, p. 37.

29. TV Turn-off Network Web site, at www.tvturnoff.org, viewed 3 May 2003.

30. Karen Lewis, Program Director, TV Turn-off Week, Washington, DC, conversation with author, 6 February 2006.

31. Joe Garofoli, "Gift Rift: Evangelicals Split over Plan to Ban Presents," *San Francisco Chronicle*, 24 December 2005.

Chapter 9. Mindful Investments

1. "Hindu Proverb Quotes," http://en.thinkexist.com/quotation/they_who _give_have_all_things-they_ who_withhold/162011.html, viewed 9 May 2006.

2. Fair Trade Labeling Organizations et al., "Fair Trade in Europe 2005" (Brussels: Fair Trade Advocacy Office, 2005), p. 9.

3. Rachel Farey, Business Manager, One World Shop. Glasgow, Scotland, conversation with author, 26 April 2006.

4. Ibid.

5. The Independent Sector, "Faith and Philanthropy: The Connection Between Charitable Behavior and Giving to Religion" (Washington, DC: 2003).

6. Ibid.

7. Giving USA Foundation-AAFRC Trust for Philanthropy, "Charitable

Giving Rises 5 Percent to Nearly $250 Billion in 2004," press release (Glenview, IL: 2005).

8. International Interfaith Investment Group (3iG), "Our Story," at www.3ig net.org/our_story, viewed 27 April 2006.

9. Ibid.

10. Figure of 31 percent is a Worldwatch calculation based on share of Christians who attend church weekly, from Adherents.com, "Largest Denominational Families in the U.S., 2001," www.adherents.com/rel_USA.html, viewed 25 April 2006, and on total managed investment from Social Investment Forum (SIF), "2005 Report on Socially Responsible Investing Trends in the United States: A Ten Year Review" (Washington, DC: 2006), pp. 1–2. Total value of managed portfolios was $24.4 trillion. Given that 80 percent of Americans are Christians, this assumes they have 80 percent of the total value, or $19.5 trillion. With 31 percent of these Christians attending church weekly, they are assumed to hold 31 percent of the total Christian wealth, or about $6 trillion.

11. Betsy Brill, "Preparing for the Intergenerational Transfer of Wealth: Opportunities and Strategies for Advisors," Journal of Practical Estate Planning, April-May 2003, pp. 25–34.

12. Estimate of $10 trillion is a Worldwatch calculation based on share of Christians who attend church weekly, from Adherents.com, op. cit. note 10, and on intergenerational transfer from Brill, op. cit. note 11. Total intergenerational wealth transfer is estimated at $41 trillion. Given that 80 percent of Americans are Christians, this assumes they will receive 80 percent of the total value, or $32.8 trillion. With 31 percent of these Christians attending church weekly, they are assumed to be in line to receive 31 percent of the total Christian wealth, or about $10 trillion.

13. Sidebar 9–1 from the following sources: giving in 1968 and 2003 from Empty Tomb, Inc., "The Potential of the Church: World Need and Giving Potential," www.emptytomb.org/potential.html, viewed 24 April 2006; giving in 1933 from Empty Tomb, Inc., "Current Giving Data," www.emptytomb .org/research.html#Fig1, viewed 24 April 2006; $94 billion from Empty Tomb, Inc., "World Need and Giving Potential," www.emptytomb.org/poten tial.html, viewed 27 April 2006; $69 billion from United Nations Population Fund, "MDGs: Frequently Asked Questions," www.unfpa.org/icpd/qanda .htm, viewed 27 April 2006.

14. Terry Provance, Executive Director, Oikocredit USA, Washington, DC, interview with author, 26 April 2006.

15. SIF, op. cit. note 10, pp. 1–2.

16. Ibid., pp. 36–37.

17. Ibid., p. 3.

18. UK Social Investment Forum, "SRI Data," at www.uksif.org/Z/Z/Z/sri/data/index.shtml, viewed 14 April 2006.

19. Interfaith Center on Corporate Responsibility (ICCR) Web site, at www.iccr.org, viewed 2 May 2006

20. Ibid.

21. Ibid.

22. ICCR, "Investing for the Long Term: Faith Based Investors Engagement with Wal-Mart, 1993-2006" (New York: undated).

23. Co-op America, "Mutual Funds and Climate Change," at www.coopamerica.org/takeaction/mutualfunds/background.cfm, viewed 24 April 2006.

24. Co-op America, "Climate Change Resolutions and Mutual Fund Voting in 2005," at www.coopamerica.org/PDF/MutualFundClimateVoting2005.pdf.

25. Sister Patricia Wolf, Executive Director, ICCR, interview with author, 25 April 2005.

26. 3iG Web site, at www.3iGnet.org, viewed 2 May 2006.

27. Right Reverend and Right Honorable Richard Chartres, Bishop of London, address to 3iG inaugural conference, London, UK, 11 April 2005, available at www.arcworld.org/news.asp?pageID=73.

28. Mark Campanale, Head, SRI Business Development, Henderson Global Investors, presentation at 3iG inaugural conference, 11–13 April 2005.

29. Asa Tham, CEO, Global Solidarity Fund, interview with author, 28 December 2005.

30. Ibid.

31. Ibid.

32. Forest Stewardship Council United States, "What is Certification?," www.fscus.org/faqs/what_is_certification.php, viewed 23 December 2005.

33. Tham, op. cit. note 29.

34. Microcredit Summit Campaign, "State of the Microcredit Summit Campaign," www.microcreditsummit.org/pubs/reports/socr/index.html, viewed 6 May 2006.

35. Terry Provance, Executive Director, Oikocredit USA, Washington, DC, conversation with author, 25 April 2006.

36. Figure of $325 million from Terry Provance, Executive Director, Oikocredit USA, Washington, DC, e-mail to author, 30 April 2006; 20 countries from Oikocredit, "Support Associations," www.oikocredit.org/site/en/doc.phtml?p =Support+Associations2, viewed 25 April 2006; 32 countries from Oikocredit, "Focus Countries," www.oikocredit.org/site/en/doc.phtml?p=Focus+countries, viewed 25 April 2006.

37. Worldwatch estimate based on the following: Oikocredit investing countries from Oikocredit, "Support Associations," ibid.; religious adherents from Adherents.com, "Religion by Location Index," www.adherents.com/adhloc/indexWhere.html, viewed 25 April 2006; population from U.S. Census Bureau, International Data Base, www.census.gov/ipc/www/idbsum.html, viewed 25 April 2006.

38. Ibid. Regular churchgoing refers to those who attend at least monthly. Estimate of 2,300 families obtained by dividing 239 million regular churchgoers by 26,000 regular Oikocredit investors, to yield 9,192 churchgoers who do not invest with Oikocredit. Assuming that some of these are children and spouses of potential investors, and that each family consists of four people, the number of families that could invest is 2,298 for every one that does.

39. Figure of 23 million from Terry Provance, Executive Director, Oikocredit USA, Washington, DC, e-mail to author, 25 April 2006.

40. Worldwatch estimate based on 23 million from Provance, ibid. and on $6 trillion from Worldwatch calculation, op. cit. note 10. Figure of $261,000 is arrived at by dividing $23 million into $6 trillion.

41. SIF, op. cit. note 10, pp. 1–2.

42. Ibid., pp. 28–29.

43. Community Investing Center, "The 15 or More in Community Investing Campaign," www.communityinvest.org/investors/campaign.cfm, viewed 27 April 2006.

44. Mark Howland, Head of Marketing, The Charity Bank Limited, Tonbridge, Kent, UK, e-mail to author, 19 April 2006.

45. Ibid.

46. Ibid.

47. Ibid.

Chapter 10. New Vision: Toward an Ethics of Progress

1. Wisdom Quotes, "Ethics Quotes," at www.wisdomquotes.com/cat_ethics .html, viewed 9 May 2006.

2. Rachel Carson, *Silent Spring* (Boston: Houghton Mifflin, 1962), p. 297.

3. Swimme cited in Thomas Berry, *The Great Work* (New York: Bell Tower, 1999), p. 101.

4. Berry, ibid.

5. Ibid., p. 92

6. Tu Weiming, "Beyond the Enlightenment Mentality," in Mary Evelyn Tucker and John Berthrong, eds., *Confucianism and Ecology: The Interrelation of Heaven, Earth, and Humans* (Cambridge, MA: Center for the Study of World Religions, Harvard Divinity School, 1998), p. 25.

7. Ibid., pp. 24–25.

8. Ibid., p. 5.

9. Ibid., pp. 5–8.

10. Tu Weiming, "The Ecological Turn in New Confucian Humanism," *Daedalus*, Fall 2001, p. 244.

11. Table 10–1 based on Berry, op. cit. note 3, pp. 60–65 and on Ralph Metzner, "The Emerging Ecological Worldview," in Mary Evelyn Tucker and John Grim, eds., *Worldviews and Ecology: Religion, Philosophy, and the Environment* (Maryknoll, NY: Orbis Books, 1994), pp. 163–72.

12. The Earth Charter Initiative, "Initiative Overview, Mission,and Goals," www.earthcharter.org/innerpg.cfm?id_menu=20, viewed 4 May 2006.

13. The Earth Charter Initiative, "The Earth Charter Workshop," at www.earth charter.org/files/pages/The%20Earth%20Charter%20Workshop.pdf, viewed 23 April 2006.

14. Martin Bauschke, "Toward a Global Ethic (2006)" (Tübingen: Global Ethic Foundation, 2006).

15. Tony Blair, "Values and the Power of Community," speech to the Global Ethic Foundation, Tübingen University, Tübingen, Germany, 30 June 2000.

16. Kofi Annan, "Do We Still Have Universal Values?" speech to the Global Ethic Foundation, Tübingen University, Tübingen, Germany, 12 December 2003.

17. Global Commons Institute, "Contraction and Convergence," www.gci.org .uk/contconv/cc.html, viewed 6 May 2006.

18. Rowan Williams, Archbishop of Canterbury, "Changing the Myths We Live By," environmental lecture, 5 July 2004, at www.archbishopofcanterbury .org/sermons_speeches/2004/040705.html.

19. Gustavo Gutierrez, *A Theology of Liberation* (Maryknoll, NY: 1973).

20. Bill McKibben, "Where Do We Go From Here?," *Daedalus*, Fall 2001, p. 302.

21. Ibid.

22. E.F. Schumacher, "The Age of Plenty: A Christian View," in Herman E. Daly and Kenneth N. Townsend, eds., *Valuing the Earth: Economics, Ecology, Ethics* (Cambridge, MA: MIT Press, 1996), pp. 166–67.

23. Mahatma Gandhi Foundation, "The Official Mahatma Gandhi eArchive and Reference Library, "Quotes," www.mahatma.org.in/quotes/quotes.jsp ?link=qt, viewed 7 May 2006.

Chapter 11. Getting to a New Progress

1. Walter Brueggeman, *The Prophetic Imagination* (Minneapolis, MN: Fortress Press, 1978), p. 40.

2. E.F. Schumacher, "The Age of Plenty: A Christian View," in Herman E. Daly and Kenneth N. Townsend, eds., *Valuing the Earth: Economics, Ecology, Ethics* (Cambridge, MA: MIT Press, 1996), p. 171.

3. Gould quoted in David Orr, "For the Love of Life," *Conservation Biology*, December 1992, p. 486.

4. Alliance of Religions and Conservation (ARC), "Pilgrimage Trails and Shrines," www.arcworld.org/projects.asp?projectID=65, viewed 5 May 2006.

5. ARC, "Jamyang Buddhist Garden of Contemplation," www.arcworld.org/ projects.asp?projectID=59, viewed 5 May 2006.

6. ARC, "The holy well of North Petherwyn," www.arcworld.org/projects.asp ?projectID=59, viewed 5 May 2006.

7. Mary Evelyn Tucker, *Worldly Wonder: Religions Enter their Ecological Phase* (Chicago: Open Court, 2002).

8. Madhu Khanna, "The Ritual Capsule of Durga Puja: An Ecological Perspective," in Christopher Key Chapple, and Mary Evelyn Tucker, *Hinduism and Ecology: The Intersection of Earth, Sky, and Water* (Cambridge, MA: Harvard University Press, 2000), p. 489.

9. Duane Elgin, "Voluntary Simplicity," in Allan Hunt Badiner, *Mindfulness in the Marketplace: Compassionate Responses to Consumerism* (Berkeley: Parallax Press, 2002), p. 248.

10. The Simple Living Network "Study Groups," www.simpleliving.net/study groups/default.asp, viewed 5 May 2006.

11. Ministry of Money, "Programs," www.ministryofmoney.org/Programs.htm, viewed 7 May 2006.

12. Diocese of Manchester, "Environmental Policy for the Diocese of Manchester," at www.arcworld.org/projects.asp?projectID=196, viewed 5 May 2006.

13. Jim Ball, Executive Director, Evangelical Environmental Network, Wynnewood, PA, interview with author, 25 April 2005.

14. Martin Palmer with Victoria Finlay, *Faith in Conservation: New Approaches to Religions and the Environment* (Washington, DC: World Bank, 2003), p. 61.

15. Bill McKibben, "Returning God to the Center," in Rodney Clapp, ed., *The Consuming Passion: Christianity and the Consumer Culture* (Downers Grove, IL: InterVarsity Press, 1998), p. 46.

16. Ibid., pp. 46-47.

17. Center for a New American Dream, "The New American Dream's More Fun, Less Stuff Starter Kit," www.newdream.org/publications/sk.php, viewed 5 May 2006.

18. Jim Cairns, Director, Program on Children, World Conference of Religions for Peace, New York, NY, interview with author, 21 April 2005.

19. World Council of Religions for Peace, "Mission and Activities," www.wcrp .org/RforP/MISSION_MAIN.html, viewed 7 May 2006.

20. Joan Chittister, "Understanding Spiritual Politics," address to the Conference on Spiritual Activism of the Network of Spiritual Progressives, Washington, DC, 17–20 May 2006.

21. Daniel C. Maguire, "Poverty, Population, and Sustainable Development," in Center for Development and Population Activities, "Interfaith Reflections on Women, Poverty, and Population" (Washington, DC: 1996), p. 49.

Index

About the Author

Gary T. Gardner is Director of Research at the Worldwatch Institute, where his writing has focused on nutrition, agriculture, water, materials use, and the role of religion in sustainable development. Since joining Worldwatch in 1994, he has authored chapters in the Institute's annual *State of the World* reports and contributed to *Vital Signs*, *World Watch* magazine, and the Worldwatch Paper series. Mr. Gardner does regular speaking engagements worldwide on topics as broad as "The State of the World" and as focused as global bicycle use. He also does newspaper, radio, and television interviews in English and Spanish.

Before joining Worldwatch, Mr. Gardner was project manager of the Soviet Nonproliferation Project, a research and training program run by the Monterey Institute of International Studies in California. There, he authored *Nuclear Nonproliferation: A Primer*, which is also published in Spanish and Russian. In addition, Mr. Gardner has developed training materials for the World Bank and for the Millennium Institute in Arlington, Virginia, and worked for two years on development projects in Peru.

Mr. Gardner lives in California with his family and is an active member of his local church.